HAVE LIFE YOUR WAY

LIVING YOUR WEALTHY LIFE FOREVER, WITHOUT
THE MONEY RUNNING OUT

CLAIRE SWEET

authors
AND CO.

Disclaimer: Nothing in this book should be regarded as either Financial, Legal or Tax Advice.

The Content is based on my professional knowledge and life experiences and is provided for informational purposes only. You should not construe any such information or other material as legal, tax, investment, financial, or other advice. Please do your own due diligence or seek personalised advice from an appropriate professional before taking action.

———————————

CONTENTS

1

THERE'S A HOLE IN MY BUCKET

I t's great earning good money, isn't it?

Knowing that you're having a real impact on the lives of your clients and getting paid more in a month than some people get paid in a year is just incredible. And you need to be incredibly proud of what you've achieved so far!

But in some ways, I bet you still wonder how you got here. You're just an ordinary person who decided to do something a bit different; to step out and do things your way... and it has paid dividends (literally!!)

You've reached a level of success that most people only dream of.

At first, the novelty of earning better money sent you on a spending spree, and there wasn't a week for six months when the Amazon driver wasn't banging on your door.

Me too.

But that stage doesn't last forever.

You soon realise that you've bought all the things that you said you would when you reached 6-figures and finished all the home improvements on your list.

You still have a sizable chunk of cash sitting in the bank.

And you're not sure what you should do next.

You know leaving the money sat in the bank isn't the best solution, but there are so many options out there, and you've not got time to sift through the mountain of confusing stuff online (that you suspect might be written by a random person with not much more of an idea than you have).

You're enjoying being able to take your friends out to lunch and book nicer hotels when you want to go away. One part of you feels like you'd best spend it whilst you have it, because this stage of your life might not last forever, but the other part is secretly worried that you'll fritter it away and have nothing left to show for all the money you've earned.

Somehow, the dream doesn't quite feel right, and if you had to put your finger on it, you'd probably say something like:

I just don't feel as wealthy as I thought I would, earning this kind of money.

Wow! What a thing to say... and now you feel a bit guilty too, bearing in mind that so many people earn way less than you and they seem to get on with things ok.

But the truth is, somehow, earning at this level hasn't provided the security you imagined.

You're spending far more time working than you ever planned to because it STILL doesn't feel like you're making enough money. You're terrified that it will run out, leaving you on that hamster wheel, where you think the only answer is making more money... but if you're honest with yourself, it's affecting your quality of life.

You miss out on time spent with your husband and kids.

You're on client calls in the evenings, when you'd rather be watching TV and relaxing, or going out with your friends.

You continue to hustle and grind.

You keep toiling over clients and projects that don't light you up.

And end up sneakily checking your emails in the bathroom, when you should be enjoying time with friends and family.

You tell yourself that it's just a phase. It won't be this hard forever.

That you'll ONLY do this until you sell out your next programme/have that big launch/reach some target you've set for yourself.

And then it will be ok, and you'll settle into the laptop lifestyle, travelling the world first class with your immaculately turned out (and well-behaved) children.

You just need to earn a bit more money (and you've got a coach who can help you with that) ...

Uh – uh (the booming wrong answer buzzer from Family Fortunes echoes around the room).

Time for a light-bulb moment.

I'm going to share something with you that I've learned from working in Financial Services for over 14 years, and building a multi-six figure business from scratch.

There is no magic number at which this all gets easier.

Which deep down you know, because you thought it would all feel better when you reached £5k months. But it didn't.

And reaching £10k months didn't help either.

Eventually, you'll get a blinding realisation that no matter how much money you pile in the top and no matter how many income streams you have, if you don't get the underlying stuff sorted, you'll always feel like this.

It's like trying to fill a bucket with a hole in it.

This never-ending slog to get more clients into the top of your funnel, make more sales, bank more cash.

Which means you spend nearly all your time being the worker in your business, serving clients and making sales, when you know you want to be more of a CEO, and work ON the business rather than IN it.

This certainly wasn't the picture you had in your head when you decided that working for yourself was the best option for you.

It's like you've created a job with a blood-sucking tyrant as a boss – and that person is you!

And you're not alone in that.

Society tells us that, as businesswomen, we need to do it all:

Juggle the challenges of running a successful business with meeting all the needs of your family, whilst appearing to be this calm version of Wonder Woman ready to conquer the world.

Like everyone else is doing.

But it's exhausting, isn't it?

Despite the flexibility that working for yourself brings, you still wish that you could unwind and switch off when you finish at the end of the day, like employees do when they go home, and don't give work another thought until they arrive the next day.

But your brain keeps whirring.

New ideas for your business and ways to interact with clients, that Canva subscription you forgot to cancel, and all the other things that you need to add to your ever growing to do list.

Plus, all the things you think that PROPER business owners are MEANT to do... when they're not busy doing the day job.

And then there is that worry that the money sitting in the bank account isn't doing anything except being eroded by inflation and that in ten years' time, you'll look back and wonder where that million pounds went.

What?

Maybe you've never sat down to think about money like that before.

But the truth is that if you're making 6 figures a year, then in ten years' time you'll have made a million pounds (or dollars or whatever currency you're using where you are in the world).

That's a scary thought, isn't it?

But we all know that if you don't have a plan for your money then it will just get spent on stuff. And years from now, you'll not quite remember what happened to it.

Whereas it could be effortlessly doubling in value every 6-12 years, allowing you to do more with it now, and in years to come.

Which is why we are here.

And why I've written this book.

Because I want to show you how to use your money to create security for the future, whilst enjoying an incredible quality of life, so that you can really start to enjoy the wealth that you've created, and not feel guilty about wanting to have more.

And to inspire you to come up with a sensible, sustainable strategy that means that your money is always in the right place, at the right time, and you've got no worries about it running out, even if you choose to work less hard in the future. Because, let's face it, traditional retirement is just not on the cards for you. Now that you're in a career that you love, and you work every day with clients that light you up, you're not just going to hang up your boots at 68 and watch Homes under the Hammer, are you?

So, how does that sound?

Are you ready to look at money in a different way, and have a simple and fun way to get it working for you, as hard as it can, leaving money along the way for gin, holidays and the things that make life fun?

(This is not going to be one of those personal finance books that tells you to scrimp and save, spend every penny repaying debt and make you feel guilty about how you want to spend the money you earn.)

I'm going to show you how you can take all that money that you're making and turn it into real wealth.

So that your money makes more money.

And you can take your foot off the gas a bit.

Maybe schedule some time in your diary for you to read a book, have lunch with a friend... or simply feel relaxed enough to get up from your desk for a break every so often, rather than realising 2 hours later that you still didn't go to the loo and are now busting for a wee.

A new way of living life where money becomes the tool that enables everything else to happen.

And ceases to be a source of worry or stress.

Leaving you free to live life your way... without ever worrying that the money will run out.

Meaning that you can spend your time with the people you love, doing things that matter.

And isn't that what we all want really? To enjoy life and share it with others?

Because this is what I've been doing with all my clients for the last 14 years.

Helping them to get the things in place that provide ROCK Solid ™ foundations, so that they're free to grow their wealth and build their dream, taking them from money making women to wealthy women.

(And yes, I work with men too and am fully inclusive to those of all genders and none.)

It's why I set up my financial coaching and training business to complement my role as an FCA regulated financial adviser.

One of the things that I realised with all the appointments that I'd had, helping people to buy their home or plan their retirement, was that so many people had questions about their finances. They didn't really understand how money could, or should, enhance their life, rather than being a stress-creating thing that just created confusion.

I took the time to help people organise their money, and often had people who were not ready to buy a home yet leave my office with a plan of action to save a deposit, pay off credit cards and improve their credit score - something that I did as part of a consultation at no cost to them, in the hope that when they were ready, they'd come back, and I would have the opportunity to place some business.

Making someone else's life better gave me a massive feel-good factor, and although I didn't have a way to charge for this part of what I did, it often resulted in them recommending my services to others and as it boosted my reputation, my business continued to grow.

I soon realised that there was a huge opportunity in financial education and helping people get clarity on their numbers and direction, and that people were prepared to pay for this.

Both Phil and I had management experience and had set up businesses after leaving corporate jobs and so we knew that we had the skills to help people, if only we worked out the best way to do so.

And that's where *Peace Together Money Coaching* came in – but why did I call it that?

To be honest, I needed to a name. My accountant was nagging me to set up a ltd company - a great way to reduce my tax bill, he said.

And so, my husband and I sat down with a bottle of wine to come up with something.

The *peace* bit came first – our initials.

Philip Edwin and Claire Elizabeth – but peace... what? What did I want to say to people about our business?

Together – we're in this journey together.

I didn't want to tell them what to do; I wanted to hold their hand whilst they did it.

Often, when something is scary and you need to take a step forward, you need someone to hold your hand, because sometimes what you are dealing with is a mental block rather than a physical obstacle.

When I trekked along the Great Wall of China to raise money for the hospice in 2007, lots of it wasn't like you imagine. It's not all castle on a hill stuff like you see on the TV – some of it is a little teeny path, on a 6oft wall, on top of a blasted mountain.

No safety net, no barrier, just a path you hope your clumsy size 8s will stay on.

At one point in the trek, I needed to step from one broken bit of wall to the next, across a gap of maybe 4 inches. But I was 60 feet up - frozen unable to move forward. Until the guy who was one step ahead turned around and held out his hand and I was able to relax and step forward

And so that's what I do with all my clients – reach out my hand and give them the confidence to take that step, whatever that looks like for them.

And that's what I'm going to help you do in this book.

Hold your hand as you take the first step to creating your wealthy life and the future that you deserve.

Having systems in place to ensure that I get paid a regular income every month and have a financial safety net in place is one of the greatest comforts I have as I go about my everyday life. It's meant that I've been able to grow my business and invest in myself, which in turn has meant I'm now drawing an income higher than I ever imagined possible.

I work what my family deem to be part-time. I don't work Fridays or weekends anymore and aim to be done each day to pick my son up from school. I have time to spend doing things for myself and get to spend time in the fresh air with my alpacas. And every day I get to help other women move one step closer to creating their own dream life – which is the best reward I could hope for!

Here's a glimpse into the wealth-building success that some of my clients have experienced:

Catherine's Story:
Tax Cuts and a House in the Country

"I chose to work with Claire as I really wanted to focus on creating a regular income from the business and get all my financial loose ends tied up.

She showed us how to draw our business income in a more tax efficient way, meaning that although my husband and I continued to draw the same income each month, we gained an extra £400 a month, which meant I was able to finally get a pension set up and use this money for our future (rather than paying it as tax to HMRC).

I was also able to simultaneously reduce my company's tax bill further by putting the things in place to provide the money to complete my children's private education if anything terrible happened to me (or my business partner husband).

But best of all, we were able to structure our business income so that we could buy our dream home just six months after we started working with Claire.

During one session, I made a throwaway comment about wanting to buy a house in the country but that we could never borrow enough to make the purchase... and Claire showed us how to do it without needing to increase our earnings further. Six months later we were in our dream home."

Mary's Story:
Work Less, Travel More & Retire Early

"Having run a busy business for many years, I knew it was time to reduce my client load and start to take more time off to travel and enjoy time with my family, but just couldn't see how that would work financially without me giving up doing all the things in my free time that I love.

Working together, we created a workable plan to reduce my client facing time to three working days per week and calculated that if my wealth continues to grow at the same rate, I can stop working completely at 50 and have enough income to last until I'm 94!"

They are just two examples of how understanding how your money works and the options available to you can help you achieve things you never thought possible.

And it FEELS great.

I've got many examples of clients that I've worked with over the years who I could tell you about, but I struggle to share their stories as so much of what I do remains completely confidential.

But I can tell you a bit more about me.

I left the security of a well-paid and well-respected role as a pharmacist, to retrain in financial services and set up a business from scratch, a business which now employs four staff and turns over multi 6 figures a year and allows me to live in my dream house, with a bespoke office built in my garden and a herd of eight alpacas on our 4.5 acres of land.

I draw a generous, regular income from my business each month, even if I take a couple of weeks off to sit in the sunshine. I have systems in place so that I can see at a glance the profit in my business, the growth of my assets, and have that CEO view of my finances that can only happen when you make time to step out of the day job.

But it wasn't always like this.

I once went food shopping with just a £2.50 Sainsbury's reward voucher.

I was in a new job, in a new town and wasn't earning much. It was the first time I'd had to manage all of my own money, with no-one else's salary to top up the account and a week before payday, the account was empty.

It's amazing how much shopping you can buy with £2.50 if you have to, but I don't EVER want to be in a position like that again.

So, I have the things in place behind the scenes that prevent this happening, which means that I'm free to work with the clients that I love, and build my wealth without worry that the money will run out.

I have a plan and some strategies in place and keep at them consistently and if you do the same, it's perfectly possible that you can build whatever your dream is, without the fear that your lifestyle might come crashing down around your ears at any moment.

I've helped hundreds of clients to buy their dream home, plan their comfortable retirement and create a sense of financial confidence that enables them to go about their lives without ever worrying about the money being there.

And you can have this too.

But we're going to need to deal with a few things first.

Like why the little voice in your head tells you that it's wrong to want more than you have already.

And why you're so reluctant to deal with your money stuff, or ask for help rather than soldiering on alone.

And then I'm going to share how my ROCK Solid ™ method can give you the peace of mind that you need so that you can confidently move on with living your best life and doing all those amazing things that are on your vision board, knowing that you're building your wealth on foundations that can weather any storm.

We'll cover how to get your money effortlessly working for you, both now and when you want to work less hard.

I'll explain, in straightforward terms, different investment strategies to grow your money and create lasting wealth, whilst minimising your tax bill now and in the future.

We'll look at how to structure all this so that it can adapt as your needs change, without the money running out.

I'll show you how you can free up more disposable income from the money you're already making and improve your quality of life whilst having more fun with your money (and lose spending guilt forever).

And how taking just one hour a month to keep on top of this stuff can see you celebrating your growth, month after month, whilst knowing exactly what to do with your surplus money as your business continues to grow.

This is about equipping you with a financial ideology that you can use to create intergenerational wealth... So that your family can continue to benefit from the business you've created, long after you're gone.

You'll see your money grow, your confidence soar, and you'll be truly free to live the life you love... your way!

Step by step, in straightforward and light-hearted language, I'm going to take you from money maker to wealth creator, and we'll have a bit of a giggle along the way.

A jargon-free book that will, chapter by chapter, let you know what to do next so that you feel like you're making real progress... and if you have any questions at the end, feel free to get in touch (see last chapter for the best ways to do this).

So, let's take the first step and look at what it feels like to be wealthy and how getting your head straight is the first thing that needs to happen... are you ready?

>>> (turn the page) >>>

2

IT'S OK TO ENJOY YOUR MONEY (WHATEVER THAT VOICE IN YOUR HEAD SAYS)

Last summer, I fell in love with a Kate Spade handbag that popped into my Facebook feed.

I saw it and just knew that it was THE bag for me to buy. As I clicked through the Facebook ad and ended up on the website, I was even more convinced that this was the combination of fun and stylish that I was after.

But as I browsed the website, the voice of my mother popped into my head.

"£240 and it's not even leather"

I look at the beautifully worded website description, listing the bag as a sustainable vegan leather-alternative. I realise I am considering buying a bag which is, in effect, made of plastic.

"OMG!! You can't spend THAT on a plastic bag. What other bags do they do?"

There's this lovely one in chestnut brown leather. Yes, it's a little more at £295 but it IS leather (and is therefore a quality, heirloom-style option) – now THAT would be a more sensible choice. Get that one.

But I didn't really want another grown-up, sensible bag. So, I closed the webpage and went back to the thing that I was meant to be doing before I got side-tracked by the advert in my feed.

Over the next few days, I saw MY bag everywhere I went online. Google. Facebook. Instagram. That's the thing about targeted adverts, cookies and the wonder that is the internet and the data we share. (So please bear this in mind before making a purchase that you feel some cosmic power is leading you to).

But I held my nerve and didn't buy the bag – even though I really liked it.

I'm sure you know that there are lots of things that affect how we chose to spend our money, and how we feel about money in general. Loads of this stuff is what we've been told by people we trust, adverts we've seen and research we've done. But a whole load of it is the narrative we've absorbed (often unknowingly) as a child.

I'm not going to use this book to blame all of my money habits (good and bad) on my parents, and neither should you. We're grownups and the buck stops here. But taking some time to consider the story you tell yourself about money, wealth, and spending can really help you to have a much wealthier future (and FEEL better about money).

It's a fact that we absorb a phenomenal amount of data between birth and eight years old, which is a great thing otherwise we'd never successfully learn to do things like walking, reading, swimming and all the other things that we take for granted as an adult. But we can also learn habits and beliefs that don't serve us as an adult, which we then must un-learn. The key is that we need to know what these things are, otherwise we can feel like we're pushing against an invisible wall, unable to get to where we need to, but not quite know what is holding us back.

There are lots of ways that you can look to uncover your money beliefs and I have a couple of favourites if you're looking for a way to start.

Journaling (which is just a fancy way of saying grab a piece of paper and write some things down on it) is a way to capture the conscious money thoughts. Don't try and do this on your laptop or phone, it needs to be a physical writing action to get the best results.

Use a series of headings on your piece of paper to complete the following sentences:

I want to earn amazing amounts of money because...

If I had a whole load of money I would...

Rich people are...

Money is...

Write whatever feels natural and then read back what you've written to see how you feel about it. Are you surprised by anything that you've written?

Take some time to think about when you were a child. How much money did your parents have and how did they speak about their/your money? Were you encouraged to save/spend? Did you get things that you asked for? Was life comfortable or a struggle? How did they speak about other people who had money (or didn't) and do they still have the same views?

Write down these things and anything else that comes back to you – try not to think too hard, simply start writing and let the words flow onto the paper. Then stop and read them back to yourself, preferably out loud.

This will give you a lot of understanding about your conscious money beliefs. Then you must decide if they are still true for you now that you're an adult. And if they're not, you can choose to believe something different.

Look around you and see all the opportunities that being wealthy will bring to you, your family, and the wider world - like a better standard of living for your family; never needing to worry about the money running out. Meaning that you can live life to the full and have amazing experiences which bring you joy and give you memories for years to come.

Money brings the opportunity to give generous gifts to those that you choose, to donate to charities you have a heart for or even take on some pro-bono clients who couldn't usually afford to work with you, set up a foundation, build a wing at a hospital, or create a project that you are passionate about to have a massive impact in the world.

You can ONLY do these things if you're earning good money AND using it wisely to create lasting wealth – otherwise you'll have nothing left for your own spending.

Which is what happens to so many lottery winners. One day they're broke, then they win millions and within five years, most of them are broke again. They've never got their head straight about money, let alone got any systems or processes in place.

But what about the subconscious stuff?

Now, without going all woo woo, there are several ways that you can do this – either on your own, or with the help of a trusted friend or therapist. Deep down, you know the answers, you simply need to bring them to the surface and listen to your own intuition.

Your brain wants you to feel safe and will often lock away things that were painful for you or things that it thinks might cause harm. But the problem is, that what was scary to 6-year-old you... probably isn't a problem for you as a grown up. This often distorts the meaning of things because at the time, your brain couldn't understand what was happening or why, but you carry this feeling, thought or fear into adulthood without realising.

If you're looking for a way to find these answers without help from a therapist, you need to find a way to trigger that knee jerk reaction- where you say what's in your head without putting a filter in place.

Like the time when I accidentally called my teenage daughter fat, much to my horror (and hers). But then, I've never said that I was a perfect parent!

I bet you're wondering how on earth that happened?

We were discussing inny and outie belly buttons (of all things) in one of those random post-dinner conversations that happens when you also happen to have a 10-year-old.

My son and I have outies. My husband has an inny. My daughter said she can't tell... I said "that's because..." well, let's just say it wasn't my finest hour.

But my point is, that when you say the unfiltered thing and it just comes out, you get the REAL answer.

What does this mean for your money story and that internal narrative?

If you're not one of those people who can generate answers by talking to yourself and asking questions out loud (or as part of a journaling exercise as above), you can enlist a trusted friend to bombard you with questions, Mallet's Mallet style, until you say that thing that you really mean. Get your friend to ask you a series of questions about money and wealth in quick succession, which you answer with the first thing that comes into your head. No pausing, no hesitating... you remember how the show went, right??

Repeating the questions in random order and increasing in speed and intensity until your mouth blurts out the thing that your brain thinks is important. It's possible to have more than one OMG moment during this process.

Now, I'm not a money mindset specialist (although I can recommend one to you if needed) and this is very much the surface level stuff, but it will set you on a path of self-discovery which will hopefully lead you to choose some professional support at some point to move deeper onto the next layer of discovery and healing.

Money mindset, money blocks, upper limit issues, inner voice, whatever you want to call it... it's an ongoing process, not a one-and-done thing. So be prepared to revisit this regularly throughout your wealth journey.

The professional option

One way to uncover the inner voice is to use a therapist that you trust to use a hypnotherapy-type process to access the memories of your past and become aware of the things that are holding you back. This is something I've done several times when I've felt like there is a block to my next level of success. The revelations and learnings that come out are often really surprising. I'm happy to share some of the things that I discovered during my healing sessions with you, to illustrate the profound long-term effect that seemingly average experiences can have on your life, business and wealth.

We're not necessarily talking about abuse or serious trauma situations here. I had a pretty average childhood, but still managed to accumulate some baggage which affected my ability to spend money on myself. Logically, I could buy the bag. I had the money in my account and buying it wasn't going to affect my ability to pay my bills or anything... so, what was stopping me? The inner voice that had been triggered by a childhood experience and my mum's attitude to money when I was growing up.

So, what was this pivotal memory? Must've been something super traumatic, eh?

Nope. When I was five, we went shoe shopping. I wanted the pretty pink shoes, but my mum bought me the ugly brown ones. My child-self took this to mean that I can't buy fun things; I need to use my money to buy the sensible, practical option. Nuts, right?!

In the same situation, I'd have made the same choice as my mother. Although at this point of my life we had a bit more money to spend on stuff than when my parents got divorced (due to how my mum spent/managed her money rather than due to how much financial support she got) we only ever had one pair of leather Start-Rite shoes (plus trainers/wellies/sandals etc.). You've seen how much kid's leather shoes cost – I'm sure price per inch they work out more than most designer brands!

Now, I can look back and see how little-me took this to mean 'we don't buy fun/frivolous/colourful things' we buy the safe/sensible option – and how for years this affected my purchasing choices.

But I'm now aware of the pattern, and know that it is no longer relevant or useful to me as an adult. Using this knowledge, I can *consciously* choose to buy the things that I love (as long as they fit my spending plan) rather than buying the safe option on *autopilot*.

So, I HAVE bought the bag – and loved using it all through the summer!

I was initially surprised to find that some of the things that affect how you deal with your money don't necessarily relate to money-related issues in your past. The links can be really tenuous but have a profound effect.

The biggest one that I uncovered was a memory that I actually do remember but had no idea how the impact of it had affected my life for so long, from the age of 3 years old until really quite recently.

I remember shortly after my sister was born, standing in the smallest bedroom of our three-bedroom home (with her cot in front of the window), looking at this little baby soundly asleep. My mum asked me "shall we call her Michelle or Lorraine?" ... I chose Lorraine. My parents chose the other name. So, I obviously can't be TRUSTED to make the right decisions in life.

This was a big one for me.

It led me to spend all of my childhood, and many of my adult years, seeking approval from others (especially people in authority, parents, teachers, business coaches) to make decisions in my life and business, rather than listening to myself and what I really wanted. You can read more about this part of my story in When Women Heal, the charity book project that I co-wrote in 2021 (link at the back of the book).

This lack of self-trust also meant that when making decisions, especially about finance, money and spending, I used to spend hours doing research - looking in to all the options, weighing up all the benefits, reading online reviews, asking others' opinions – terrified that I'd make the wrong choice. Frozen from taking action by reading webpage after webpage, rather than jumping in and buying the thing that I needed, worried that I made the wrong choice.

Trust is a big issue for many of my clients too. You need to trust that you can make money, keep money, and spend money wisely. Trust that there is more money to come, and that you can make those choices that will enable you to have the life you love and build a legacy for the future.

Learn to TRUST yourself and suddenly everything changes, your confidence improves, and you can start to move forward. If you don't, you'll find a distraction technique or tell yourself you're not good with money, so that you have a reason to not take action to build your wealth.

So, even if you're not a particularly woo woo person, I'd urge you to do some mindset work at some point, as it will make your path to wealth easier. Which is what we all want really. But there are also some practical ways to allow you guilt free spending, which you can be working on at the same time (or instead of, if you're not at the right point in your journey to do the mindset work yet).

Let's look at some incredibly simple practical things that I do with all my clients, whether they're on my foundation programme ROCK Solid TM or working with me in my premium 1-2-1 experiences.

And this is the first practical step you can take towards guilt-free spending.

Money Pots.

I was first introduced to the idea of money pots when I was gifted the book The Wealth Chef by the very first business coach I worked with in 2011. It's not a new concept; you might know it as the envelope system and in all likelihood will have come across it in some way before.

The idea is that when your money comes in (wages/business drawings) you separate the funds out into different categories based on what purpose that money has. Like as a teenager when you first saved up to buy that jacket/computer game/first holiday away with your friends... each time you got paid from your part-time job (or got your allowance) you put some of it in a piggy bank to save for what you wanted.

We're going to bring this concept into the adult world and use it to enable you to spend, guilt-free, on those things you really want. It also means making sure your bills get paid on time and you always have the money in place for those big annual costs, like Christmas and a decent summer holiday.

What we're going to do is set up some separate bank accounts rather than having everything come in and out of one account every month. If you bank with a modern bank, you may be able to set up separate pots of money within your main account, but I'd still suggest setting up at least one extra actual bank account (you'll find out why in a moment).

Having more than one account (or pot) allows you to cate-gorise your spending so that you can easily see what is avail-able to spend, without needing to do a budget planner (unless you want to – you can find a link to the one I use at the end of the book in the resources section).

How many accounts you have is up to you, and I often get asked how many to use. Like most things, there's no right or wrong answer, but here's a few things to help you decide.

Personally, I use six bank accounts, but as a minimum you're going to need three.

One pot is for bills & direct debits or must haves.
For most people this will be your usual current account,
where your mortgage and direct debits get paid from already.
Keeping the money for these essential costs separate means
you don't risk spending it by mistake. This can avoid direct
debits bouncing (incurring bank fees or leading you into your
expensive overdraft) and stop issues with your credit file if you
miss payments on credit cards or loans.

**One pot is for nonessential spending or nice to
haves.** I call this my fun stuff account and use it to pay for
things that make our quality of life better. Having a separate
account for this discretionary spending can really help
prevent overspending as you can see how much you have
available and make smart buying choices - when it's gone, it's
gone! Make sure this account has a debit card that you can use
to pay for your meals out and other fun things, so that you can
clearly see how much is left until you next top the account up.

**Plus, you'll need one for 'your dream fund', that
thing you really want to achieve** (we'll come on to that in
chapter 4). This doesn't need to be a current account, it could be a
savings account (or even the NS&I premium bonds) as you'll be
putting money in regularly, but won't need access to the money
that often. Even if you're currently repaying debts, you should still
have a small amount of money going in regularly to this pot. Even
if you can only afford £1 a week, it will soon build to allow you to
move towards that thing you want and give you something to look
forward to... rather than only looking back at debt from the past.

You can have more accounts than this if that is what works for you. The key thing is, if something is really important to you, a pot is created for it. Then the money is ring-fenced so that it's spent on the right things and not frittered on stuff or spent in the supermarket on groceries.

You might have a pot for mountain biking because you need to have money available to buy bikes, pay for repairs and upgrades, competition entries plus the necessary overnight stays for training events, etc.

You might have a pot for clothes, shoes, and bags because you really love fashion and want to have good quality items that will last for years.

You might have a separate account for holidays, or to save for a new car, or for the deposit for a second property. Money, like time can only be spent once, so choose what YOU want to allocate it to.

I have 6 pots in total, and lots of my clients choose something similar. Each month, I allocate a fixed percentage of my drawings to each, and the money moves automatically the day after payday.

I'll tell you a bit more about how I do it in chapter 5.

I've been managing my money like this since 2012 and it allows me to feel confident that the money is available to pay my bills, whilst allowing me to spend freely on other things that are important to me.

So, now you've got your head straight and you feel comfortable spending your money, and have a pot of money allocated to use, it's time to step out and buy those things that you've been putting off for ages!!

Now you can spend guilt-free on whatever you want to (as long as you have the money in the right pot to do so).

But won't it feel weird spending money on these lovely things whilst some of your oldest friends manage day-to-day on much less money than you do? Many of them only earn a year what you can earn in a couple of months! What would they think if you buy the £240 bag or spend £700 on a pair of shoes?

I'd like to think that your true friends will be supportive, excited and happy to share in your success. But that's not always the case and this is often because they have their own inner work to do. It can be hard to watch someone else's success if you've not been brave enough to follow your own dream, and some of them will display this with jealousy, sarcasm or simply ignoring your achievements.

This means that it might be time to let these people gently drift away, so that you spend less of your week with them and instead seek to surround yourself with other successful women who want to live a wealthy life. (You'll find these women in higher-level masterminds and group programmes and at networking events aimed at people like you). I'm not saying to cut yourself off from your friends and family, simply to ensure that you're limiting the time spent with people who are unsupportive, indifferent or not excited to be part of your future.

> "You are the average of the 5 people you spend the most time with"
>
> — JIM ROHN

It's time to normalise women being successful in business and in life, and using their money to create wealth to benefit them and the world around them.

And that's what I want to do with this book and programmes like Magnetic Wealth™ . Bring together incredible women who each have a vision of a better future, so that they can gain the knowledge and support that they need to be truly free to live the life they love...

But first, let's chat about what's stopped you moving forward on this before now...

3

THE OSTRICH

When looking to use this chapter to discuss why we avoid dealing with our money stuff, the obvious metaphor was that of an ostrich. Head in the sand, hoping that his predator can't see him and his problems will all vanish. So, I thought at this point I'd put in an ostrich joke, as an attempt to lighten the mood and reassure you that this is not another mind-numbing finance book lecturing you on what you've done (or not done) so far.

Want to know the best joke I found?

> **Q.** Why is an Ostrich wealthy?
> **A.** Because otherwise it would be an Ostpoor...

I know, a bit lame, but it made me smile, which was the point here. And it was the cleanest joke that popped into my search listings that wasn't overtly sexist or misogynistic.

So, have you got a good picture of an ostrich in your head? A huge flightless bird, often featured in cartoons for the sheer comedy value, whose two survival strategies in life consist of either running away or burying its head in the sand. The typical flight or freeze response.

I've never been one for running which, bearing in mind I'm gangly and uncoordinated and run like Phoebe out of Friends, is quite understandable. I'm sure in a time of danger I could run if I had to, and I'd just have to hope that I could outrun my companions, even if I couldn't outrun the bear. So instead, I'd probably choose to cover my eyes with my hands, like a toddler playing hide-and-seek, and avoid looking at that thing looming towards me. Like the ostrich.

But the thing to remember is that although the ostrich thinks he's safe, nothing could be further from the truth. Now his head is buried in the sand, he can't see the lion eying up his juicy rump (like Alex did to Marty in Madagascar), which puts him in even more danger than looking the lion straight in the eyes.

All childish cartoon metaphors aside, we can only deal with problems if we face them head on - trying to avoid them doesn't help you in the long run. And that includes getting your financial ducks in a row and having your money work for you to be able to create effortless wealth.

I want to reassure you that your reluctance to tackle this is understandable and it's not your fault you don't have it all figured out yet! You're not taught this in school, well I certainly wasn't. The sum total of our money education in the 1990s was learning how to write a cheque (not a particularly useful skill these days) and being told NEVER to get a credit card. No-one explained to us that we'd get taxed on our earnings when we started work, that we needed to save for our retirement or what a credit score was (let alone how to keep it intact).

And let's face it, the business coaches you've worked with focus on helping you to grow your business and make more money. None of them show you what you should do with the money you've made. So, it sits there in your account doing nothing and you feel guilty that you're not putting it to work, but you don't want to risk losing it by making the wrong choice.

You've heard people your age talking about pensions, Profit First and building property portfolios. Some of your friends are raving about bitcoin. You're at the stage where you're ready to take action on this grown-up stuff, but you're not sure which bit to tackle first as you look at this big mountain that we'll call your financial stuff. And, like any other mountain to conquer, when you're looking at it from ground zero it feels huge and you have no idea how you'll ever get to the top of it. Which means that for many people, it causes them enough stress and anxiety that they add it to their to-do list along with doing the ironing or booking their smear test and find ways to avoid taking any action at all.

It's time to change that. And eat the elephant.

You've heard that saying, right?

> **Q.** How do you eat an elephant?
> **A.** One bite at a time.

The same goes for any other important task in your life or business, including your finances. You only need to take one step at a time towards your goal and when you look back; you'll be surprised just how far you've come.

Walking the Great Wall of China was an incredible achievement in my life, although it was a physically and emotionally gruelling experience. The uneven surface (and whacking great drop) meant that you spent a lot of the time looking down at the next step you were taking, and not admiring the view. From time to time, we'd stop for a break and, as you looked back along the tiny white line that ran along the top of the mountain, snaking off into the distance, you were able to marvel at what you'd achieved. I've walked ALL of that today! Wow! I never managed to take a photo that really captured the magnitude of the situation.

Life can be like that too. We get so caught up in doing the day job and living our life that we don't always realise the progress that we've made. It's one of the reasons that regular reviews are so important (I'll cover that in chapter 8) – and why so many business owners book in regular time to work on their business, rather than in it, even if that means booking a night in a hotel so they can focus.

I'm going to tell you later how I can help you carve out this time in your diary and ensure that you take action on those things that you need to do (without you feeling like you're at school or having to spend time doing things that don't move you personally forward).

In the next part of this book, I'm going to help you through my ROCK Solid ™ process, step by step. This will show you what you need to be looking at so that things run smoothly behind the scenes and you can get on with living your best life, whilst enjoying your business and doing the things that you are good at.

I know that a little part of you isn't even sure what you'll find when you dig into it, and that's ok.

I know that you want to do it right (and not mess it up) and that is where this book will allow me to hold your hand as you increase your knowledge, start to understand your options and make the best financial choices that you can at this present moment in time.

And then you can come back and do other things as and when the time is right to do so, or if your circumstances change.

But there's one thing that I really need you to understand...

This is your individual journey, and it will be completely different from most people you know, even those who are in business at a similar level to you. Because that's the thing about money, it's personal. We're going to build on what you have in place already, and you're all starting at different places, with a different end point in mind.

So, you need to ignore what you THINK other successful business owners are spending their money on and investing their money in and avoid jumping onto a bandwagon without seeing if and how it fits into your personal wealth plan.

Social media means that we see pictures of holidays, new homes and lifestyles that seem amazing and think that they must have everything bottomed out. But if we're honest, we know that only the best pictures make the camera roll and that all may not be as it seems.

So be reassured that beneath the many curated images of elegant swans upon a lake of financial confidence, many successful business owners are furiously paddling to prevent capsizing.

I've seen 7 figure entrepreneurs who have no idea how much profit their business makes (although they'll be posting all over their socials about how big their latest launch is). I've also worked with more than one 6 figure entrepreneur that had to use their own personal savings to pay their staff wages bill when an invoice wasn't paid on time and they had a dip in their cash flow.

So, just as no one puts on the post where their kiddy sliced his leg open at the beach after being told 100 times not to climb on the breakwater, or of the dog puking on granny's antique rug, you can be pretty sure that EVERYONE does not have all their financial things running as smoothly as you'd think. And you are NOT alone in wanting to get things sorted.

As someone who works with all manner of businesses every day, I've seen some stuff that will make your head spin. Let me reassure you, you are not even half as bad as you might think; focus on your own journey and forget what you THINK others are doing with theirs.

This isn't about complicated, time-consuming tasks. I understand that you're so busy juggling your life and business, that you don't even have time for lunch most days. This is about focusing your effort on the few key things that will have the biggest impact: working through a step-by-step process so that you can see the progress you're making and be inspired to continue, without feeling overwhelmed, to tackle those things that provide peace of mind and allow you to focus on living your best life now, and being able to plan for the future in a way that works for you. Not some cookie-cutter, one-size fits no-one approach.

Money brings choices, and it's now up to you to find out what options you have, and then use them to create a plan that has a balance of money for now, and wealth for the future, so that you can confidently hire staff to support you in your business, and know that paying their salaries long-term is sustainable. Allowing you to book holidays where you stay in the hotel you really want, not just the cheapest one that *will do*. Giving you flexibility to work part-time, pick your kids up from school and not miss out on time with your friends because you're desperate to fill your diary with client calls.

Most business strategists and coaches that you've come across so far will tell you that you just need to earn more money, and then all of these problems will disappear. But that isn't the case, and I'm sure you've realised that by now.

They'll tell you that to have a consistent monthly income, you need to set up an online membership or course with a payment plan. That the ONLY way to have flexibility of time in your business is to step away from the 1-2-1 model and look at a group/one-to-many approach.

But for some people, this isn't the way that they give the best value and most significant outcomes to their clients, and trying to implement a group model just brings the frustration of trying to fit a square peg in a round hole. That feeling that everyone else is, and so I should too. They don't understand that you'd rather work in depth with four £25k clients a year, or run exclusive events. They tell you that this is not the way to scale your business and that it will be impossible to get consistent income if you go down the route you've chosen (It's not... I'll tell you how you can do it in chapter 5).

The key thing is that it doesn't matter how many income streams you have, and how much money flows into your life; if you don't get the underlying stuff sorted, you'll always feel like you're struggling and have this desire to keep chasing the next big thing. Which, let's face it, is exhausting.

It's time to stop and enjoy life. And realise that you've got enough money to start living your dream life now and that you can start to FEEL better about your finances as you continue to grow your wealth. It's time to be able to confidently chat to your accountant about your plans and understand how the numbers in your business contribute to your overall success, So that when you meet with them to discuss your figures, you can see that not only have you made more sales this year than the year before, you're also really growing your wealth.

So why should you trust me to help you with this?

I've been in the finance industry since 2006 and have built a business based on trust, integrity and customer loyalty. We've survived the things that world has thrown at us to blossom into a thriving and progressive business, employing four staff (two of which joined us during the pandemic).

I'm a fully qualified and FCA regulated financial adviser, with all the certificates and letters after my name that you'd expect. I've been recognised and won awards for Customer Service and Best Caring and Supportive Business, plus I was the Best Business Woman Financial Services Winner in 2018. It is formal recognition that transparency, responsibility and care for clients are indeed at the heart of my business, where new clients come to us purely through recommendation and we frequently have a considerable waiting list for a new client appointment.

But running my coaching and training business and working actively in the online world means that I bring a new and refreshing approach to financial management (and about as far away from the stereotypical image of a financial adviser as a bloke in a suit that you can get).

Traditional financial planning only works if you have consistent income. It just doesn't fit with the ups and downs of income when you operate a launch-based model; in fact, it's true to say that most financial planners probably don't even know what a launch is, never mind the fact that it only has a 1-in-5 chance of success.

They don't understand that it's not about being full-time or part-time, and that business in the online world is different. You could put hours into your next launch, and be working yourself to the bone, and it can still flop, and leave you hanging without any income.

Traditional Financial advisers want you to have a way that makes sure the money doesn't run out, but they're going about it wrong for people like us. They'll tell you to set up insurance to ensure you get paid if you're too ill to work, because they're used to working with employees and owners of bricks and mortar businesses, where getting paid is all about how many hours you sit at your desk. They don't realise that you're building multiple streams of income, some of which passively ping into your stripe account, whether you're off sick or not.

These experts may tell you to repay your mortgage early and save for your retirement, but they frequently overlook that you want to have an amazing quality of life, which gets better every year, even as you make progress towards your big goals. And that you'll never really stop working, now that you've found your purpose and the career that you love.

I know that you want flexibility and freedom... as well as financial security.

And the way that I work with my clients allows them to do exactly this.

Working 1-2-1 we really take time to connect. I get to find out what really matters about where you are and where you're headed and then can use my combination of professional knowledge and life experience to help you create the best path forward to that future you desire.

And you can rest assured that I'm the most open-minded person you could ever hope to chat this stuff through with. You'll never get told off for what you've left undone or made to feel unworthy when the secret chaos of your money stuff is exposed.

And you can continue to post about your successes on social media, knowing that I never post about clients I'm working with (unless they do so publicly first), so your privacy and confidentiality are assured at all times.

I'm someone who understands the journey you're on because I've been there too. Married 3 times, divorced twice, a single parent, bereaved, countless house moves before finding my dream home. Starting a business from scratch and trying to reconcile all the stuff that I thought I knew about money from my days in the corporate world, with the reality of being an entrepreneur and being responsible for doing it all.

Which means that not only am I someone you dare to trust with your financial secrets, I can really understand the frustrations with dealing with something that isn't in your zone of genius, but really needs to be something that you've got on top of.

Trust me, I know how it feels to be too exhausted in the evenings to do more work or attend a training session. I also know that there's no point you sitting through another 90-minute webinar promising you the earth, but that doesn't produce results because you don't have time to implement what you need to move forward.

In part two of the book, we're going to look at the solution, by helping you to get clear on the bigger picture and then giving you actionable tasks that will get your money working effortlessly for you and provide the security that you crave.

Plus, I'll be able to share with you more of my journey, so that you can see if I can have life my way, then you can too.

So, let's move to the next chapter and start taking action.

4

THE BIGGER PICTURE

L ike so many of us in business, I love a good vision board. It's an incredibly effective way to get clarity and focus on your goals.

As my lovely friend (and epic business coach) Leigh Howes says, "you wouldn't get on a bus, without a destination on the front of it."

Sounds quite simple really, but you'd be surprised how many people wander around in a daze, living life as it comes with no direction or purpose. Which means they don't get anywhere fast.

When we get clear about what we want – the physical things, people in our lives and how we want to feel – we become naturally drawn to the opportunities that support our vision and push us towards our goals. Which is amazing, when you stop to think about it!

Now, before you think I've gone all woo-woo on you, I should point out that there is scientific basis to this. After all, I am a scientist at heart and like logical explanations where possible (you know I originally qualified as a pharmacist and then changed careers into financial services), and I have always found the way that our brain works to be completely fascinating!

Ever found that when you buy a new car, every road you drive on has the same model of car on it? Or how when you're pregnant, everywhere you look there are other pregnant ladies?

That's your Reticular Activating System (RAS). The part of your brain that looks out for things to support your belief – to validate that you've made the right choice. There is so much information bombarding us on a daily basis that our brains filter out the things that it thinks are more useful to us - to show us the things it thinks we need or want to see.

Sometimes this is called confirmation bias – if you've had a good experience with something, you'll subconsciously look for ways to validate your experience. In effect, your head looks for ways to justify those internal/gut-based decisions by showing you the 'evidence' to support your choice.

But this can work the other way too. If you believe that rich people are arrogant, your subconscious will look for arrogant rich people to show you and let the generous, philanthropic rich people slide past un-noticed. So, it's really important that we tell our brains to look for the right things.

This is scientifically how a vision board works.

By getting clear on what you really want to achieve in your life, your Reticular Activating System will do its magic and you will find that you are more focussed on spotting the opportunities that will bring you nearer to those things that you desire.

A great way to do this is by creating a vision board. If you've never made a vision board before, it's pretty simple. You take a board (or a big sheet of paper will do) stick it up on your wall and cover it with pictures of everything you want to do, be and have in your life. There are also tools to do this online. I often ask my clients to create a secret board using Pinterest. This allows them to share it with me during our planning session but keep it private from their online audience.

But there is a KEY part of this process that many people miss.

We can't just make a vision board and expect it all to drop into our laps, otherwise I'd be sat here with George Clooney and a jar of chocolate spread...

You're going to need to put a plan in place for each of your objectives and take a little step each day towards at least one of them. Putting your vision down on paper is really powerful, but taking ACTION is the important part.

Clients sometimes tell me that this can seem massively overwhelming at first and they don't know how to start – which should they start with and why? You know that expression you can't see the wood for the trees?

The danger is that left unsupported, they may end up doing nothing. They are so close to having an amazing change occur in their life but just need to get started.

I help them work out which one is really the most important picture to them (and the real reason why) and then we get started on that one. As we celebrate the tiny milestones along the way, this gives them confidence to start on others. Some we park for now, and when we check-in together further down the line, they see that some of them they have moved towards as if by magic. There is no magic. They've become so clear on what they want to achieve and why, that their subconscious works WITH them to help them get there.

Your subconscious is so important – and it's why it's so important that you've let go of any limiting beliefs on success, becoming wealthy or having things go right in your life. If you've skipped ahead in this book, then pop back to chapter 2 and work through some of the exercises there. Take this opportunity to unpack the stuff in your head and get clear on what is really true for you and what is not.

So, let's move on to the activated vision boarding process that I use with my clients and how you can use it to feel like you're making progress towards your goals.

Step #1: Get clear on EXACTLY what you want to achieve.

The first step is always getting a crystal-clear picture of what you want. Use your vision board to create a really vivid picture of how you want your life to be.

So, jump onto Pinterest, or grab some magazines and a Pritt stick and glue some pictures onto a big piece of paper and start to pull together your vision board. Find images that really capture the things that you want to aim for, rather than choosing the first one you see.

- Aim for 9-12 things in total
- A mixture of things to buy, experiences to have and feelings you want to create
- Make it balanced for business and personal goals
- What do you REALLY want to achieve?

Try to make it balanced so that you have things that benefit your business and your personal life. If you've included things for your partner or children, make sure that you include some things for yourself too.

The important thing here is to really look at each picture and see how each of these things makes you feel, as this is the REAL thing that you're trying to achieve, and the thing that you need to be focusing on. The new car you want, is it about HAVING the car, or about how it will feel to drive it? That people will see you drive past and admire your achievement?

That the leather interior smells so nice it makes you feel like you are a success and that you are truly wealthy?

Spend some time looking at the pictures you have chosen and concentrate on how they make you feel, and imagine what your life would be like as the person who HAS that now. If the picture doesn't evoke the right feeling, go back and find a better example – you'll know it when you find it!

Your board shouldn't just be a shopping list of things you want to buy (although it's great to add on that car or those Manolos if you want to). You should think about the person you want to be, the experiences you want to have and the places you want to go as well.

On my vision board I have a picture of a lady with arms outstretched, walking in the sunshine which to me represents health and fitness. She gets outside regularly to enjoy the fresh air, smiles, and laughs and is vibrant and full of energy. This picture spurs me on to take action to improve my health and become the fit, active and well-nourished woman that I want to be.

I also have a picture of a lady sitting under a tree, reading a book. I've been told that is an odd choice, bearing in mind I have 4.5 acres of land and a massive assortment of books. Surely, I can go and read under a tree whenever I wish? Yes and no. This picture represents calm which, for me, is definitely a work towards.

So, for me to sit under the tree and read a book, I'd need to know that my business can run largely without me, with a team that can keep the wheels turning when I take time out. I'd need to know that I have a constant influx of ideal clients enrolling in my programmes and can pull a generous income from my business. I'd need to know that my housework is taken care of and that my husband and children have all they need.

As I said. It's a work in progress.

Taking time to create a vision board is well worth doing, and it can be extremely therapeutic to get the scissors and glue out and stick things to a piece of paper, or something physical. My current board came from the amazing Sarah Stone, and is a creative Feng Shui ® Intentional Vision Board. I was really attracted to the design and it's on the wall in my office with some incredible pictures stuck to it.

Put your vision board where you can see it every day. On the wall, as a screensaver on your laptop or phone – whatever makes most sense for you now.

Once you've done your board, you need to choose which ONE of the things on it you'll focus on first, and make sure you're moving forward significantly in that plan before you try to start anything else.

'Focus' = Follow One Course Until Successful.

I'm sure you've heard that before! But there's a whole lot of truth to it.

Most people choose to start with one of the smaller or easier ones. Others start on the one that lights them up most. Or the biggest one, so that you can really feel like you've started on the ultimate goal.

The choice is yours, but for now, please pick ONE of them, and make sure you are well on your way with your plan before you shift your focus away from that first goal on your vision board onto anything else.

———

Step #2. How much money do you need? And by when?

Now that you're clear as you can be about the thing you want and why you want it, you'll need to see how much it will cost you. In effect, the next step is to put a timeline on it, so you know when you want to achieve it by and how much money it will take.

Do you need the money in a lump? Or a set amount each year?

Is it one big lump? Or a bit now to get started, and then a bigger lump to scale, further down the line?

Do your research, rather than assuming what you think it will cost.

If the amount you need ends up being more than you thought, it can be really demotivating and knock you off track.

Or if it's actually going to cost less than you thought, then your vision board will be able to happen a whole lot faster!

Step #3. Finding the money.

I'm a great believer in a budget planner. If you don't have one already, you can download the one I use for FREE from your book resources section (check in the next steps chapter at the end of the book!). The reason that I love using this version with my clients is that it will add up the numbers for you AND easily separate your expenses into essential and non-essential costs.

But there is more than one way to skin a cat (so they say) so if you'd prefer, you can do it on a budgeting app or on a bit of A4 paper.

- Add up how much money you have coming in each month (every penny, from all sources).
- Deduct all your essentials like food, bills, direct debits and petrol.
- Deduct money for the nice to have stuff like clothes, meals out and haircuts.
- And then deduct anything other big things you pay for once a year (Christmas, summer holidays, car

insurance etc.) – divide the amount by 12 and add it to your budget planner.

All being well, when you take the outgoing off the incoming, you should have some money left over.

It might be £30, £200 or £900.

The actual figure doesn't matter at this stage, but now you have some money to put towards the things on your vision board.

The things in your life that are MOST important to you.

If your budget planner shows a negative figure, you're not alone! We need to chat about getting it resolved for you asap look in the back of the book for details of the best ways to reach me.

Step #4. Once you have found this 'spare' money, how much of it do you want to put towards your dream?

A third? Half? All of it?

Here's one way to figure it out:

- If you don't have an emergency fund, put 50% towards that and 50% in your dream fund. There's nothing more demotivating than needing to raid your dream fund, because your car needs a new exhaust or the boiler breaks down!

- If you have consumer debt (credit cards, loans or overdrafts), use 1/3 to clear your debt, 1/3 into your emergency fund and 1/3 into your dream fund.
- If you're one of those financially organised people who already has 3-6 months living expenses in a savings account and no consumer debt, divert all of it into your dream fund if you want to!

For each of these savings goals, you'll need a separate account or 'money pot'.

So, either open a new account with your bank (easy to do online), or dig out the details of an old account that you never got around to closing and use that.

Step #5. AUTOMATE IT!

Set up an automated payment (standing order) on THE DAY YOU GET PAID, into your big dream account – before you can spend it on a new pair of shoes or a takeaway pizza.

If you're also building up an emergency fund or repaying debt, set up automated payments for these too. This will make you financially stronger on autopilot every single month.

Even if it's only a few pounds to start with, it soon starts to add up!

This is part of what I do with all my one-to-one clients. It's about creating the habits and systems, which build towards your dream and help you take REAL control of your money.

Step #6: Milestones and Markers!

Honestly, I can't stress Step #6 enough – how important it is to put some milestones and markers in place, as you work towards your goals.

Not just so you know if you're on track to achieve them (or rather, if you're veering off track so you can steer yourself back on) but because each milestone is a mini win you can celebrate along the way!

When you feel like you're making progress towards your goals, it's so much easier to stay focused and motivated!

So how does that work in practice?

I'm going to give you two examples so that you can see how to use this process on whichever things have made it to your vision board.

Example 1

So, let's revisit that image of George Clooney and the jar of chocolate spread.

If this is something that I REALLY want to achieve, I'm going to need to explore all of the solutions that have the potential to achieve my goal and then decide which ONE I'm going to follow. Then I'll create a plan which clearly allows me to track my progress and see if I'm moving closer to that goal over time.

So, in this (purely hypothetical) example:

Options:

- Try to lure him for a romantic liaison – unlikely to work, he's married (and so am I)
- Ask him to be a brand ambassador for a well-known brand of chocolate spread and then come up with creative ideas for TV adverts – I have no relevant PR/Marketing contacts, and what I have in mind isn't going to make it to ITV before the watershed.
- Look to arrange a charity fundraiser with sponsorship and ask him, if I can raise £xxxx, will he let me have my chocolate spread moment.

Option 3 seems like the most viable option so far. But I'm going to need to take further steps to work out EXACTLY what my first steps, and next steps, need to be.

So here goes:

- Research charities that are close to his heart or he already supports and see if they'll support our request in order to raise further funds.
- Create a proposal, explaining benefits to him, the charity and my role in this...
- Submit it to his PR team, personal assistant etc., or post about it on his Twitter account
- See if I have any mutual connections online, directly with him or anyone in his team who can put in a good word for me or arrange a meeting/phone interview.

In terms of the plan, we then set objectives to spend a certain amount of time on this project each week (knowing that, as long as we are doing productive things and not wasting time staring at pictures on google, we will move closer our goal).

We create a target for the number of emails/tweets to send a day, or number of pages of a proposal to write.

AND THEN WE GET ON AND DO IT.

The point is, once you've worked out what needs to happen and in what order, it's time to take action to help yourself move along the timeline you've set.

Your plan needs to be flexible and be able to adapt as the situation evolves as often, other steps will appear along the way which will necessitate a new action plan and target to be set.

For example, once I've made contact with the right person and George's team have agreed to my request, they may stipulate that to take part I need to raise £300,000 in sponsorship for his charity.

Which means that I now have a new goal, and need to create a new action plan (with markers along the way to monitor my progress)... not that I've given this subject much thought, you understand...

Ok, that's enough of the vivid pictures! Let's look at a more realistic example that's likely to be more relevant to the readers of this book.

Example 2.

For lots of business owners, the next big goal is moving into your dream home.

It's something you really, REALLY want – all that space; light flooding in; close to amazing schools or the sea or with a pool for the kids (whatever it looks like for you!).

You've spent hours on Rightmove, it's on your vision board and you know how much you'll need to spend.

So, if you want to bring that dream home into reach, let's see what you need to do!

I'll share with you the process that we went through when we decided that we wanted to buy a home with land so that we could get our own small herd of alpacas. It took us a couple of years to get things in place so that we were able to buy this amazing house we now call home!

Firstly, you'll need to work out how much deposit you have available and where it will come from.

It might be from the house you're living in now, that you'll sell to raise the deposit. Or from savings you've been putting away, money you've inherited or money that's currently within your business that you'll pull out as a dividend.

Next, it's getting clear on how much you can borrow if you're going to want a mortgage to finance your dream home. So, you'll need to speak to a financial adviser who specialises in working with business owners to find out how much you can borrow, based on the income you have.

Sometimes you can also use retained profits in your business to boost the amount you can borrow. This is why I'd always recommend speaking to a whole of market mortgage adviser who has access to the full range of banks and building societies. (Most high street banks won't let you use retained profits!).

It's also worth talking to your accountant at this point, even if it still feels like early days in the process. Tell them you're planning the move and ask them to make sure your accounts accurately reflect the amount of money flowing through your business and that your paperwork is ready promptly.

Once you know how much money you can borrow, and how big your deposit is, you'll know if you'll be in a position to afford that dream home.

And if not? If the figures this year won't be sufficient?

Ask your Financial Adviser what your income needs to be, to get the mortgage you want.

Then you can work backwards from there. Work out what your turnover in your business needs to be to create that level of income, to demonstrate your affordability for the mortgage to buy the house you want.

In some cases, it needs to be a plan for two years, three years or even further down the line, depending on how many years' accounts you need and what your figures look like now **but the point is, if you don't know, you don't know. Tracking it is vital.**

It's about working out where you are now; where you want to get to and the plan to get there.

Taking action is the MOST important step, and often this becomes easier if you have someone along the way to hold your hand. This is why I offer all of my clients ways that we can continue to work together over 6-12 months, so that once they're created their wealth plan, I can support them to actually get things implemented and move along their timeline, ticking off the milestones as they reach them.

If this is something that you want support with, be reassured that I'll be in your corner every step of the way, supporting you to turn your vision and your dreams into your reality... however unusual your dream may be.

Get clear; set a timeline; know your plan; take action and get the accountability to make it happen.

And if you need help arranging a mortgage for your dream home, then we can help you with that too.

So, I bet you're wondering what's on my current board (now that I have the dream home and the alpacas)?

A truly balanced picture of how I want my life to look. Coffee with friends, recognition and success in my business, a London pied-a-terre and me - fit, healthy and full of energy; time for me – outside and calm in nature; holidays all over the world, entertaining and hosting events; time together as a couple and time together as a family.

Is it happening?

Yes, bit by bit. I'm building my dream, not waiting for it to happen. Not wishing the universe to drop it in my lap. And you can do the same too.

Now you know how much money you'll need and by when.

So, the next chapter talks about getting your money WORKING for you, so that you can reach your goals more quickly. >>>

5

GETTING YOUR MONEY WORKING EFFORTLESSLY FOR YOU

W hen I was a kid, my mum said that if she won the lottery that she'd put the £1million in the bank and live off the interest.

Times have changed – and I'm sure she couldn't have imagined anyone winning more than £1million, or that leaving it in the bank would pay only £100-£1000 interest per year.

So let me tell you why this is a problem for us these days.

When I was a child (in the 1980s), the Bank of England Base Rate, which directly affects mortgage interest rates, was between 8.5% and 17%. This, in turn, meant savings rates ranged from about 6.5% to 13.8%. So that £million in the bank would have generated interest of at least £65k a year, which was much, much more than our household income.

So why don't you get that interest on your savings these days?

Interest rates are at a historic low...which is great for those of us with mortgages - imagine how high your mortgage payment would be if rates were at the 1980s level now.... Or run the maths on this if you're that geeky type***.

...But that means savers don't get a decent return on their savings. Why?

In simple terms, the money that savers deposit in the bank is used to lend out to mortgage borrowers... and the lender passes on a share of the interest charged as a reward for leaving your money on deposit. Except they're not getting much interest in the top end (due to low interest rates) so choose to pass on very little of it (0.1-0.01%) on to the savers.

So, living off the interest IF you win the lottery (even if you win £14million) really isn't going to support your lifestyle... unless you can live on £1400 a year. And that's before we consider inflation, which is eating away at the purchasing power of your money. So, in real terms, if you're not getting a 2% or more return on your money, then you're actually losing money. So that £million in the bank, will only be 'worth' £980k next year in terms of what you can purchase with it. Yes £20k dropping off the value in a single year, and then it continues to drop year after year ...£960k...£941k...£922k... £903k...

So, after 5 years, the buying power of your money will have reduced by nearly £100k because the price of the things you buy goes up each year – the bank statement will still say £1 million.

And THIS is why we don't leave money we'll want in the long-term in cash. Yes, we keep our tax money, emergency fund and money that we'll need in the next few years in savings, but the rest of our monthly surplus needs to be invested so that it grows to match or beat inflation.

Makes sense?

> *** in case you're wondering, on a £200k mortgage over 25 years... in 2020 at 1.5% you'd pay £800 per month... in the 1980s you'd be paying £1351-2800 A MONTH....

But how do you work out how much is surplus, and what you can invest without leaving yourself short each month? Especially as a business owner, where your income is all over the place; I mean, it's not like you get paid a regular income like an employee is it?

NEWSFLASH- you don't NEED a membership or an online course to get paid a regular and consistent amount each month!

We all realise that, as a business owner, turnover goes up and down. I had 4 times the income in August than I got last month, and so far this month (12 days in), I'm somewhere between the two.

But come payday, I'll still get paid my regular income – the same as I have each month for the last 12 months. Which means that my mortgage and bills get paid, and all the money pings into my separate accounts so that I can live my life the way I love.

There's no stress over money, no robbing Peter to pay Paul or mad panic over how quickly people sign up to work with me. Because I've done something uncommon. And you can do this too. It takes 10 minutes and will completely change how you feel about that roller-coaster ride that is the variable income of a business owner.

Ready? Hold your hat...

Go into your business account and set up a standing order (automated payment) for a fixed amount of drawings to be paid into your personal account each month so that you create a payday...like you had as an employee.

There you have it. Consistent income EVERY month... and not a recurring payment plan in sight.

As a business owner you have a whole load of responsibility, because the buck stops with you. But you also have complete choice and flexibility to implement systems and ways of working that work for you. Which means if you want to earn a regular amount each month, then it's up to you to set it up - which in the days of internet banking, is a 10-minute job.

Choose an amount that is sensible for your business, that you KNOW you can pay yourself every month (even on a quiet month), set your payment up and then leave it alone.

Next month, if your business brings in WAY more than you expect, you still take your regular payment... which then gives you a surplus in your account that means, should you have a month that you go on holiday, or don't launch ... you still get paid your regular drawings at the end of the month.

3 or 4 times a year, take the time to look at the surplus you've created (which might be considerable if your business is rapidly growing) and increase you standing order by a small amount. For example, increase it by £300-500 a month, leave it 3 months and then put it up again.

The point is that drawing £2000 a month EVERY month will make your home financial life much calmer than taking £3000 this month, £500 the following month and£2500 the month after that, allowing you to dramatically reduce financial stress at home. This, in turn, leads to a more harmonious household.

I show my clients how to organise their business income so that they have money set aside for tax and build up a surplus of funds in a specific account that means that they still get paid the same amount, whatever happens with sales this month.

And this single step can really take them from feeling like they're in financial chaos into a place of calm in a really short space of time. Effectively, we use a simplified version of Profit

First, which is an incredible book by Mike Michalowicz that turns the whole definition of profit on its head. Not only does it make complete sense, it slots in amazingly well with the way that I already organise my personal spending (which we'll come onto shortly).

The problem with many businesses is that as they grow, the spending/costs get out of control, and this means that there is very little or no profit left at the end of the month for you to pay your own salary.

Using a system like Profit First means that you can see at a glance where your money is and what you have to spend, which means you feel dramatically less stressed and bothered about the inevitable ups and downs of your business income.

So how does Profit First work? Let me give you a simple step-by-step way to get your head around it...

Here we go.

Each month, go through your bank accounts and add up the amount that has come in from clients (having a separate account is the easiest way to do this, but not essential).

From this, put 15% in a separate account for your tax (plus the 20% VAT if this is applicable to you). You should always put your money for your tax away first. This is not your money, it never was! Remember that as an employee, your tax is taken out BEFORE you can spend it on anything else – as a business owner, you need to do the same.

In most cases, 15% of your gross incoming should be sufficient to pay your corporation tax (19% on profit once your accountant has deducted your allowable expenses). Depending on your profit margin, it may also have enough to pay your personal tax bill too. If you've got a surplus in this pot at the end of the year, you have options in how you choose to spend it. How about re-investing half into your business and buy that expensive piece of kit you wanted/work with a coach or mentor that you've been dying to partner with? – Or take half as an additional dividend, and treat yourself to something, or leave it where it is so that you can take an extended holiday next year!

Put 55% of what is left into an account which you call owner's pay. I've chosen to combine the profit (5%) and owners pay (50%) pot, because I'm the sole director/shareholder and like most UK directors, take small salary and the rest of my income as dividends as it's more tax-efficient.

In the USA, directors tend to take a higher salary which they live off and then take lower dividends on an ad hoc basis, which is why running Profit First exactly as written seems so hard for UK business owners.

That leaves 30% for your operating expenses that you can use for your staff costs, internet and other business running costs.

But how does that actually help? Surely that just leaves me even less in my expenses account? Yes and no.

All being well, this will help you to manage your business expenses and stop you from spending too much, too soon (which is really common as your business grows rapidly). You'll be able to see at a glance how much you have available to invest in that latest thing you want - whether that be a Canva subscription, a new laptop or a mentorship/mastermind costing several thousands.

I've seen this single step highlight to a business owner that they need to rein things in a bit, and allow the money to come in before jumping in to the next stage of their growth programme. It's also so much clearer what you're spending out for things you need longer need or use - much easier than looking at your profit and loss statement (after all, most of us don't look at that every day).

But the real magic happens in the owner's pay account.

Remember we're paying in 55% of the incoming? Out of that you pay yourself a regular monthly wage, so that you get the same each month as an automated payment. This works wonders for your home life peace of mind, when you can budget properly for your spending because you have a regular income source.

But when you set your payment, you're not taking the whole 55% that comes into the account. You're going to do an amount of about 2/3 of this. So, if the money that hits your owners pay account each month is £6000, you'd set yourself to get paid £4000... and leave the other £2000 sat there.

This means after three months you'll have a slush fund of £6000... enough to pay your own pay, and 2k of business expenses if you need to. Most of my clients aim to keep about three month's salary money in this account, and they usually achieve this within six months of us working together.

Once the amount in the account exceeds this safety net, you can give yourself a (small) pay-rise. Maybe increase your payment to £4500 and then wait 3 months and see what the surplus looks like. Regularly checking in on your finances and making little tweaks is crucial, and I'll chat more about that in chapter 8.

But the point is, you now have money you can use if your income takes a dip, or you take a couple of week's holiday (we're all longing for that right now...)

Plus, you have all the money you need for your taxes (with a bit spare) in your tax account, so you'll feel organised and never have to worry about how to find your tax money.

And the great thing is, that surplus in your owner's pay account doesn't NEED to be used for your wages. You could use it to pay into your pension, or invest in a coaching or mentoring programme that you've been longing for, but not sure where you'd find the money.

You could use it to pay yourself, your spouse or your child some tax-free dividends (ask your accountant about alphabet shareholders).

You could use this money to buy the new phone or laptop you want - as you KNOW it really is spare money and you don't need it to pay your staff costs!

Yes, I know that's a lot of *coulds*. But the point is that YOU choose how to allocate your money according to what is important to you. Take Michalowicz's system and tweak it to make it work for you!

To run a system like Profit First well, it does mean that you need four business accounts, or four pots within your business account (if you have that option). Your outgoings/expenses account will need to be a current account, so that you can make bill payments/direct debits and have a debit card to buy things. Most business owners use their original business account for this, so that they don't need to set up all their direct debits again.

Your tax money can be a savings account, or many business owners like to put it somewhere safe (and out of sight) like the NSandI Premium Bonds, hoping that they win a prize (which will be greater than any interest they may have gained leaving it in a savings account).

Your incoming money account can be a current/savings account, and so can your owner's pay account as these only need to accept incoming payments, and manual transfers out/withdrawals.

I trust myself to not dip into the pots, so I keep them on my standard business banking platform, so that any money transferred is instant.

If you think you might be tempted to spend out of them, then hold your tax money and owner's pay accounts at a bank without internet access, so you have to physically go into the town to take out the money.

The key thing is that once you've set up your four accounts and made sure that all your incoming money comes into the same account, you only move the money to your different accounts once or twice a month.

It's crucial that you only spend from your operating expenses account and don't borrow from the other pots unless it's an emergency. THIS is how you keep your expenses under control, and resist the temptation to buy ALL the things. Overspending on expenses is the main reason that business owners don't take the salary that they should...

So, now that you have organised your business accounts, you'll be able to pay yourself that sustainable regular income coming in each month. Which means that you can use a similar system with your personal bank accounts to ensure that your bills always get paid, and you don't spend hours each month juggling money.

Which will enable you to have two foreign holidays a year and a collection of red-soled shoes, if that's what you wish – plus create a pot of money that you can use for INVESTMENT, which is the real way to grow your money and create lasting wealth.

It's time to talk a bit more about personal Money pots.

In chapter 3 we talked about putting put some money aside for your dream, and the other things that are important to you, in separate bank accounts so that you can make sure the money doesn't get spent on something else by mistake.

We're now going to see how you can expand on this further and create an automated money management system that allows for complete flexibility in spending, plus creates a dedicated pot that you know you can AFFORD to invest every month.

I'm not one of these people who categorises their spending into different parts, just so that they can live a restrictive lifestyle. What I DO have is a system that means I can spend money, without needing to worry, and I NEVER feel guilty about treating myself and my family to the nice things.

So, although I keep a record of everything I spend - I have spreadsheets showing how much I've spent each month on food or petrol, going back several years - I don't actively budget for it anymore. Instead, I manage my money using money pots, because it gives me more freedom.

Let me explain!

There was a time when I'd go to the supermarket with £50 for my weekly shopping. I'd walk around, adding everything up to the exact penny as I went. Because if I got to the checkout and

I was running short – which happened more than once - I'd have to put things back.

If you've ever been there too, you'll know how mortifying that can feel.

It's not like that now. Now, I manage my money by running 6 different bank accounts, because that's what works for me, and you can create money pots to meet your objectives too.

Here's how to make it work for you!

From the regular income you're drawing from your business, you transfer set proportions out into different accounts, which are used for different purposes.

We've already talked about a simplified version using three of them.

One pot for bills & direct debits, or "must haves";

One for non-essential spending, or "nice to haves";

Plus, one for 'your dream fund', that thing you really want (remember your vision board?)

For many of my clients, setting up these three pots is the first step of their guilt-free spending journey. It allows them to get used to what it feels like to be in control of their money, but in a non-restrictive way. Then, they add further pots in as they get used to the idea of ring-fencing money for specific purposes.

How I do it.

As I said, I use six bank accounts, and have since 2012. Each month, the day after payday, my money gets automatically pinged out into my different accounts, which I then use for my spending.

10% goes into **Pot #1** - to INVEST for the future and build my dream. This is the account I use to pay into my ISA and my other investments. There's the £10-odd that goes on the People's Postcode Lottery, plus other savings plans and things for the future, for me and the children.

Pot #2 is for fun stuff! For me, that's usually eating out, weekends away and lunch with the girls. Plus nice skincare products and other stuff that improves our quality of life and allows us to have fun.

Again, I put in 10% of my earnings into this pot. When I go out, it's the card for this account that I use. When it's gone, it's gone. But the thing is, it's never gone! Because once it's in one place and you can see clearly what you've got, you make active choices.

Like *"do I want to spend £15 on junk food? Or would I rather spend that same money on a lovely meal out with my husband/treat myself to that gorgeous smelling candle/order that luxury shampoo?"* ·

One great thing from lockdown was that my fun stuff account built up a bit, because everywhere was shut and we didn't go anywhere. It's meant we've had some really nice weekends away since. For example, it's allowed us to go out for meals and both have a drink because we booked a taxi both ways, without having to worry about the cost. We used some of the money to upgrade our return flights to business class and have a nicer long-haul travel experience.

The great thing is that, because it's money you've allocated for fun stuff and isn't needed for bills and costs, you never feel guilty about spending it!

Pot #3 is the account I use to put money away for the big expenses every year. I put 10% in this account too.

The kids' bus pass. New school uniform. Car insurance, pet booster vaccinations, Christmas, our summer holiday… some people call this a *sinking fund*. By putting this money away each month, it means I've always got the money when the time comes around to pay out again.

Pot #4 is my charitable giving pot, 5% goes in here. Allowing me to generously give to charities I support and to our church. This also means that when one of my friends is fundraising, I have money set aside ready to donate generously and encourage them on their journey towards their target.

Pot #5 is the 10% that I use for personal development. This is money put aside for things I want to do for myself or my family so that we can be the best possible versions of ourselves in all areas of our lives. It pays for my son's karate, my husband's piano lessons and things for me like health supplements or getting my hair and nails done, because it makes me feel good.

So that leaves us with the last one – **Pot #6** - which is where the other 55% ends up. This is my current account, that pays for the bills and home running costs that I NEED to ensure get paid every month. Mortgage, utilities, petrol, food. All our everyday spending comes out of this account (either directly or by paying off - in full - my Amex at the end of the month so that I can collect reward points along the way). It's worth having an overdraft facility on this account, even if you don't use it, to prevent any missed or returned payments should you have a temporary money hiccup.

By organising my money this way, I don't have to worry about budgeting. I know the money in my current account is for bills and my food shopping. I know the money in my fun stuff account is for fun stuff.

With apps on our phones, we can keep an eye on it with just a fingertip, at any moment. It's getting these things done, and the basics organised, that gives you freedom. The feeling of KNOWING I can spend what you want, without having to worry about it, that's what makes me feel calm, relaxed, and in control.

So, it's up to you to decide where to allocate your money each month...

You can have the luxuries in your life, go on holiday and still buy gin – all while building that security for you and your family... And you can choose how much to put in each pot on a monthly basis. You could have a pot for holidays, or designer shoes. One for music concerts and theatre trips. Or one for all your mountain biking kit/bike servicing and upgrades. You have the ultimate flexibility to create something that feels right for you.

And remember, nothing is set in stone. You can always add another pot later, or merge two together. From time to time, you should check there is enough in each pot to meet your goals, which will usually be apparent if you frequently need to borrow money from another pot before the end of the month.

If you're with a modern bank – like Tide, or Starling, or Monzo – you can have one single current account split into multiple money pots, all managed with one bank card and an app.

You can even call the money pots whatever you like ('Santorini Fund') and add photos, to make them super personal – think back to that thing on your vision board that you're going to tackle first, create a pot for it and call it something inspirational! The disadvantage with this is that at a cashpoint you won't be able to see how much is in each pot (you'd need to check your app) and you can overspend without realising as you'll never get your card declined or a payment refused.

I'm with Lloyds and the old-fashioned banks don't yet offer a pot facility, so that's why I have 6 accounts! I've been with them such a long time, the service is good and the app is great, so I'm not looking to change now. The advantage of separate accounts is separate debit cards and that if you need to dip into another pot, you need to physically transfer the money from one account to another. This additional step provides thinking time to decide if this purchase is as ESSENTIAL as you think.

Whether you have multiple accounts or money pots, the system I use works in the exact same way.

It ensures that your bills get paid without you needing to juggle money, and that you can buy that handbag (even if it is £240) without feeling guilty... how amazing is that!!?

Ok, I've decided which pots I need and set them up – what now?

Choose how much to put in each pot on a monthly basis.

You can choose a fixed amount each month that you've calculated from a budget planner or simply use a percentage of your income. This is my preferred option as it ensures that as you start to earn more, you allocate more to fun, your dream and all of your other categories so that your standard of living can increase and you don't end up spending more of it on bills (or leave it sat in your current account doing nothing).

So, what does this look like?

If you're drawing an income of £4000 a month... you'd set up automated payments each month of:

£400 to your dream fund

£400 to your fun stuff

£200 to your charity pot

£400 to personal development

£400 to your annual spending pot

Which leaves £2,200 in your bills account.

You may choose to use different percentages than me, it depends on what your household income looks like against your expenditure – you need to find something that is workable and you can stick to. If 10% of your incoming won't cover your annual spending -the example above would give you £4800 over the year for Christmas gifts, summer holidays, car/home insurance, car service etc. -then you need to pick a percentage that works for you and reduce or eliminate one of the other pots.

The great thing is that once you've set up something that works for you, it can be left to run on autopilot, leaving you to focus on the more important things in life.

Money is the tool which allows you to achieve what you want, but it needn't be the focus of your thoughts on a daily basis!

So that's the *organising* your money bit done, let's move on to something equally important >>>

6

YOUR COMFORT BLANKET

I t's time to talk about putting some things in place and covering some of life's what ifs. I'm going to continue in my light-hearted manner but please be assured that this is such an important thing for you to do for your family and those that you love.

So, let's say this is the chapter that deals with the things that make up what has traditionally been thought of as your safety net. But I'm here to put a slightly different spin on it, and besides, Comfort blanket is the term I've used in my ROCK Solid™ programme... the acronym wouldn't work otherwise!

One of the Premises of ROCK Solid™, and the way that I work with all my clients, is that you need to deal with the foundational stuff before starting to build your wealth. And now that I've shown you how to create that regular income, and organised your bank accounts and spending goals, it's time for us to tidy up those other loose ends too.

There's an old-fashioned expression in the financial adviser world, used when considering family insurance plans, which is "Kids can't eat bricks".

We use this to mean you can't tie up all your money in assets (property/pensions etc.). There must be money available for those emergencies that crop up. And, heaven forbid, if something horrendous should happen to you. You've probably got something in place to repay the mortgage if you die, but how are your family going to feed themselves if you're no longer around to provide an income?

Not a pleasant subject to consider, but death comes to us all. Being properly prepared means that in a time of grief, your family aren't left in the sh*t . They can get on with dealing with their emotions, supporting each other etc., without worrying about how to pay for the funeral, or if your kids will need to leave their prestigious schools.

So, I'm going to ask you to consider what happens if you die... and what happens if you don't.

In practice, your comfort blanket is going to contain a mixture of savings and insurances, and exactly what you need is going to depend on your own personal circumstances. I'm going to explain the benefits of each option, so that you can decide the best way forward. If you'd like some personalised advice, you can book in for a free protection review (see chapter 9 for how to book an appointment) and I can design a plan that works exactly for your needs. But for now, the key thing is to see what you already have in place and identify where the gaps might be.

So, why is it so crucial to sort these things out?

Because no-one else is going to. Seriously, as a home-owner and business owner, you're going to be entitled to very little or no state support should you become ill, unable to work, or die.

But the good news is that you can make some good decisions NOW and, with minimal tweaks over the next few years, have something that will last you as long as you need – and possibly save you some tax too – whilst providing peace of mind for you and your family.

So, let's deal with the one that is certain first.

What's worse than dying and leaving your family heartbroken?

Leaving them heartbroken, without enough money to pay for your funeral and a paperwork nightmare to deal with. You never imagine that this will happen, but I've seen it more than once in my 14 years as a financial adviser.

We often put off getting our affairs in order as we don't want to tempt fate - leaving it sat on the 'to do list' for years. But the consequences of inaction can be dreadful - after all, does anyone really want their loved ones to be crowdfunding for their funeral?

It can seem like there are so many loose ends to tidy up that you often don't know where to start - and so you put it off for another day. But the day has to come at some point. They say there are only two certainties in life - death and taxes... and there is no way to avoid the former! If we're honest, we'd like to think that we wouldn't cause more stress at a time of mourning by leaving the family wondering how they will feed themselves or pay for a funeral at such an emotional time, but this is going to mean giving it some thought now, AND putting the things in place that you need.

So, what do you need to consider if you want your family to have the freedom to grieve in peace, without financial or paperwork stress?

I've created a handy checklist, which you can download from the resources section, so that you can come back to this topic more than once if you need to, but I'm going to go through the five most important things to do (if you've not done them already).

Write a Will.

You'll need to specify who will be your executors and be responsible for filling out the probate forms and allocating your estate according to your wishes. Most people choose their reliable best friend or sibling but whoever you choose, it needs to be someone you trust to follow out your wishes when you're gone. Someone who can follow a set process and fill out forms in the right order – you'll need at least two executors in total and one may be your spouse if you like (but doesn't need to be).

You should take this opportunity to also name guardians for your underage children. This means in event of the death of both parents, they can stay with the person(s) of your choice rather than becoming a 'ward of court' and ending up in foster care whilst your family apply for residency.

Yes, you read that right. The kids don't just 'end up at Grandma's house' if you die without a will – they may end up living with strangers at a really upsetting time, whilst your family apply for residency... and we all know that court-related paperwork is not ever speedily processed.

Your Will also allows you to say if you'd like to make any specific gifts to friends, family or charities and then who you would like to pass the rest of your estate to. So, if you've always planned for your best friend to get your leather jacket or your cousin to get the family heirloom jewellery this is your chance to say, and leave no doubt as to your wishes.

Do not assume that without a Will, your spouse gets everything (they usually don't) or that your unmarried partner will be entitled to anything at all. The rules are complex on this, and vary depending on where in the UK (or the world) you live at the time of your death.

You might be able to get a basic Will written for free from your bank, or if you're part of a Trades Union. Or you can seek assistance from a solicitor or licenced Will Writer. Some financial advisers arrange Wills for their clients through a partnership with a local firm.

Legally, you can write your own will on a piece of paper, providing you fulfil all the necessary wording and witnessing requirements, but in my experience, it's easy to make simple mistakes which might make the Will invalid or open to challenge after your death. For the sake of a few hundred pounds, it's worth doing things properly.

You should remember to review your Will if your circumstances change – especially if you're planning to get married as this may invalidate your current Will (undoing all your hard work in one go!)

Review your Life Cover

Ensure you have enough life cover to repay any debts you have (mortgage/loans/credit cards), plus consider whether you need a lump sum for a surviving spouse to take time off work to care for the children.

Would YOU have additional childcare costs, or need to work part-time in your business if something were to happen to your partner? Never underestimate the value of a non-earning spouse in allowing you to run your life and business the way that you do.

Most people set up protection plans to cover their mortgage, but what about all those other costs that your family has each month? Do you need to cover those? Remember, your kids

can't eat bricks. It may be that your partner's income is sufficient to cover it all, or that they have savings to fall back on,
but have you actually done the maths to check?

If there is a shortfall then some additional life cover is a good
idea, either as a lump sum, or an income to pay the household
bills until your children are grown up and out of school.
Ideally, you'd want your policies set up in trust so that in event
of your death they can be paid quickly (without waiting for
probate), and so that they fall outside of your estate for inheritance tax purposes. If you're not sure if yours are in trust,
they're probably not. You may be able to put them in trust
later, but if not, you may want to use this as a reason to look at
redoing your cover.

If possible, you want to set up your life cover in a tax-efficient
way, so if you're a Ltd. company director, ask your financial
adviser if your business can provide some life cover for your
family if you die. There are specific plans designed to do this,
and they're deductible from your corporation tax, if structured
properly from the beginning (you can't just pay your existing
personal life cover from your business account).

How will they pay for your funeral?

Even arrangements for a basic ceremony are likely to cost
more than £6000 – and depending on your wishes and location, might be a lot more than this.

Give some thought to how your executors will pay this cost as it will need to be paid before they are granted probate and can sell your property etc.

Do you have savings set aside for this, or a pre-paid funeral plan? Or should you top up your life cover to provide money that can be used? The answer will depend on your individual circumstances but you'll need one of these, or a combination, to ensure the money is ready when needed.

What happens to your business when you die?

Do you have savings held in your business to pay your staff wages in lieu of notice if the company closes down and cannot run without you?

Or is there money to recruit someone to take on your role so the company can continue to trade?

What happens to the clients you are currently working with? Do they get refunds? Where is the money for this?

If you're the only breadwinner, will your partner need to go back to work?

Will your spouse inherit your shares, or do you plan to leave them to someone else – this may be really important if you're in business with someone else. Would your partner want to run the business with your best friend? Or do you need to ensure your friend has funds available to buy back your shares from your spouse, so that she can retain control of the business?

Where do you keep your important stuff?

Keep a file that contains all the information about the investments and assets you hold, plus the log in details for your online accounts, in a safe place that your executors can access after your death.

This is especially important if you've always taken responsibility for the financial things - does your partner know the answers to the security questions to access joint accounts or utilities? Sounds simple, but not knowing this may cause a whole load of stress at a difficult time and mean unnecessary heartache.

Covering off these 5 essential topics, and then periodically checking in on them to make sure that what you've put in place still meets your needs, is a MASSIVE step towards avoiding leaving a mess behind when you die.

Are you still with me?

I realise that it's a bit of a serious topic and maybe you want to take some time out to relax, recharge and do something that will make you smile before we start talking about the maybes.

So, now on to an equally cheery topic - What if you don't die?

Statistically you've got a 1 in 13 chance of dying before you retire. But you've a 1 in 6 chance of being off sick for more than 6 months, and between a 1 in 3 and 1 in 2 chance of getting cancer in your lifetime (depending on which study you read).

So, it means that putting things in place for illness and loss of income is even more important than thinking about what happens if you die.

Again, each of you reading this will have a different outlook on life and view on this, but on the whole, there are four things that go hand in hand with the points that we covered above.

Lasting Powers of Attorney

A lasting power of attorney (LPA) is a legal document that lets you (the 'donor') appoint one or more people (known as 'attorneys') to help you make decisions or to make decisions on your behalf.

This gives you more control over what happens to you if you have an accident or an illness and cannot make your own decisions (you 'lack mental capacity'). Any adult over the age of 18, who is of sound mind, can set up a power of attorney. You do not need to live in the UK or be a British citizen to set one up.

There are two types:

Health and Welfare - This gives your chosen attorney or attorneys the power to make decisions about things like:

- Your daily routine, for example washing, dressing, eating.
- Medical care.
- Moving into a care home.
- Life-sustaining treatment.

It can only be used when you are unable to make your own decisions. It can be useful if you think that your next of kin might not make the decisions you'd want and you want to appoint someone else to make those decisions instead. It can also be useful if family members are likely to disagree about medical decisions, which could cause problems – for example, if some would want to switch off life support, and others wouldn't – you can appoint an attorney who you know will follow your wishes.

This is really important as if you go into a nursing home without one in place, then the state (as represented by the home manager/social services) decides on the care provided and the family cannot opt out of treatment or remove you from the nursing home without their consent (for example).

Property and Financial Affairs - This gives your chosen attorney or attorneys to power to make decisions about money and property for you, for example;

- Managing a bank or building society account.
- Paying bills.
- Collecting benefits or a pension.
- Selling your home.

It can be used as soon as it is registered, with your permission.

Although often thought of as a tool to help elderly relatives, they have other uses too, including short-term incapacity (extended hospital stay or prolonged illness). They can also be really useful for people who travel a lot and are away from home and need someone to act for them – especially if it involves documents to be signed that cannot be done electronically. They are also useful if mobility stops the donor from going to a bank/council office as it allows the attorney to sign documents and act on their behalf.

When setting one up you can choose to make one type or both.

It currently costs £82 to register a Lasting Power of Attorney, to complete and submit your LPA online using the gov.uk online tool - although there are some reductions or exemptions on this cost, so worth double checking if you are eligible. Solicitors can also submit them on your behalf, but the cost is likely to be around £500 (plus registration fee) each.

You can cancel your Lasting Power of Attorney if you no longer need it or want to make a new one, providing you still have the mental capacity to do so.

Insurance

The amount of insurance that you'll need will depend on how much money you have in emergency savings, the types of income streams that you have and whether you have any financial dependents.

I know we've already spoken about life cover, but what about all the yukky stuff that USED to kill people, that now probably won't due to early detection and advances in medical science? Things like cancer, heart-attacks and strokes have much better survival rates than when we were children, but the effect of you (or your partner) having one of these and being out of action for some time can be massive in terms of household income.

And let's face it, if the person you love was in hospital with something horrible, you'd like to take time out of your business to be with them and your children, and not be worrying about how much money is coming in.

You may have this covered, using the reserves in your owner's pay account which will allow you to still get paid for 3-6 months, or you may have some savings at home that you can dip into. But if not (or you don't want to be reliant on your savings), you'd be sensible to speak to your financial adviser about Critical Illness cover (CIC) and/or private sick pay/Income Protection (IP) plans.

And YES, you really should get professional advice on this one. Advice is not as crucial when setting up LIFE cover as, when it comes to it, someone is either dead or they're not – which means the biggest problem you might make is choosing a company who make the claims process tedious.

When it comes to CIC and IP, the differences between the plans can be phenomenal and some cover things that others don't, or allow you to claim at an earlier stage of an illness which can really be significant. Many provide additional benefits such as cover for your children, or partial payments if you have a less severe cancerous lump (which normally wouldn't qualify for a pay-out) – and it's fair to say that getting the best QUALITY cover needs to be your objective here, rather than picking up the cheapest option you find online.

That doesn't mean that it needs to be expensive - plans can be tailored to your budget – but you really need to be clear what you're covered for (and not). Please note that the Terminal illness cover included (for free) in most life cover plans ONLY means that if you're diagnosed with less than 12 months to live, you can have the money now to tidy up your affairs. Think of it as an accelerated death benefit – it is not the same as critical illness cover. If you're not sure what you have in place, check with your insurer or get your financial adviser to review your policy documents to check.

Critical illness plans need to be paid for personally, but there are some sick pay plans that can be paid for by your business – providing it is set up in the right way. For many business owners, this is the most important insurance they have (after their employers/liability cover) as it means that if they're off sick from work for any reason (including accidents, as opposed to illnesses) they get a monthly amount that they can use to pay their bills until they are ready to return to work.

But it's important to get the right type of cover for your needs, and that it starts paying out at the right time, so that your family isn't struggling when they'd rather be at your bedside. And that your Income protection plan pays out if you are unable to do YOUR job... not expecting for you to do one deemed suitable by the insurer instead.

A few years back, my Granny had a stroke and was in hospital for several months before being moved to a nursing home. In the bed opposite her on the stroke ward was a lady in her 30s, with a photo of her two primary school aged children Sellotaped to the side of her bedside locker so that she was able to see it without needing to move her head. In all the times that I visited my Granny, I NEVER saw this lady with any visitors. Maybe that's simply a co-incidence. Or maybe her husband had to go back to work, or had no money to pay for childcare so that he could visit his wife without bringing two little people along.

Contrast that with the experience of my friend (and client) Sadie, whose husband had a stroke when out running in November 2019. He was 36 at the time. The critical illness cover we'd put in place allowed her to repay their mortgage (which was their biggest monthly expense), which meant that she was able to take time out of work to look after him through his recovery and support their two children.

This stuff is important. And up until the point where you have sufficient passive income and/or savings, will mean a massively different outcome for your family.

Which brings us on to the final two things that make up your Comfort blanket – emergency savings and Standard Operating Procedures.

We've covered the uses for your emergency fund at several points throughout this book already, but to recap – this is a pot of money, held in cash that you can access quickly if you need to. When deciding how much you want to keep aside, you should consider how much you'd need to pay for one-off unexpected expenses (like car repairs, vet bills or a replacement boiler) if you don't have insurances /cover plans in place to cover these. You might also want money to pay for a funeral, or to pay household expenses if someone is unable to work through illness.

Take some time to think about how much would make you feel comfortable. Add up the things that you think you'd need to be able to pay for and then see how you FEEL about that amount. Is it enough? Or is there a figure that feels better?

How does that compare to what you ACTUALLY have in savings? If you've got the money already, move it to a dedicated account for this, and then you're done... except for the odd review and tweak, of course.

If you've not got what you'd like, then think about diverting some of your monthly surplus identified in chapter 5 to your emergency pot, until you reach the figure that you need.

So, where do Standard Operating Procedures fit in to all this?

Have you thought about how your business could keep going if you were temporarily unable to work through illness? As business owners, we tend to keep a lot of our knowledge in our heads and our cards close to our chest, meaning that often the things that you do, only you know how to do.

Now, obviously this depends on the type and structure of your business and whether you have an in house or outsourced support team, but by putting a few things in place, your business could run a lot more smoothly if a catastrophe were to happen.

Standard Operating Procedures (SOPs) tell the person reading them (or watching the video) how something is done in your business, and you can create them for every task that happens.

They're used massively in the corporate world, which is why you can walk into any McDonalds and get a Big Mac which looks and tastes the same. They have a process to follow which is communicated with their employees and allows consistency, whoever is at the helm, in whichever location.

If you already have a team in place, SOPs help massively with training as you can ask staff to follow the official process and only ask for help if they get stuck, allowing them autonomy and minimising interruptions in your day. In event of your illness or prolonged absence, it would allow your PA to know how you like emails responded to, how to run payroll for your staff etc. Simple things like them having access to log ins for you emails and contact details for your accountant can really make life simpler.

It's a good idea to create a disaster plan for your business, spelling out what happens to clients you are currently working with if something happens to you. Is their programme put on hold, taken over by a colleague or refunded (and if so, are there reserves in the business to cover this?)? What about notifying your clients about your situation? Who will do that and how? You don't want the first they know of your absence to be a social media post that someone shares online.

If you need help setting up things like SOPs, then look up my friend Skye Barbour. She's got some amazing resources to help.

And there we have it. The C from ROCK Solid™ fully explored, giving you the opportunity to take the ACTION that you need to create that feeling of security that you crave. Leaving you free to live your life, grow your business and grow your wealth without worry.

And remember, if you don't have a financial adviser to chat this stuff though with, you can use our contact details in chapter 9 to book in an appointment to review your protection, write your Will or chat about other ways to work together.

Hooray!! Now we've spent some time getting this stuff bottomed out, we're free to focus on the more exciting stuff – like planning your future, knowing that we won't get knocked off course if life throws us a curve ball. Here we go...

7

ONE DAY YOU'LL WANT TO WORK LESS HARD

No matter how much you love the life you're living, we all get older. And as we do, our outlook on life and priorities may change, and our health may mean that we no longer want to live a life that runs at such a fast pace. You might want to have more time with your children. Or to spend some extended time travelling the world. And at some point (as the grey hairs start to outnumber the others), you might want to do a bit less client work than you currently do.

I'm not going to refer to this stage of your life as retirement, which conjures up pictures of old people sat on the seafront with a bag of fish and chips, or a people sporting a series of dubious fashion choices – so I'm going to call it working less hard, which, after all, is why most of us went into business. The corporate world is full of people working rigid hours in a job that hopefully they like (or at least they don't hate) so that one day, they can retire and do what they really want: travel, spend time with those they care about and pursue hobbies and interests that bring them joy.

What I want to do is to help you build that life for yourself NOW, and not wait until you're too old to enjoy it. Which is where your wealth plan comes in, and why I wanted to write this book to support you.

This doesn't mean that you don't need to plan for those years when you'll be what other people call retired, but it means that you might want to go about things a bit differently so that you have flexibility further down the line if your plans change.

Business owners typically have more than one income stream. We all know it's not sensible to have all your eggs in one basket or to be reliant on a single contract or type of service. We saw that particularly over the last 2 years when the Covid 19 pandemic had an impact of some sorts on most business owners. So, a variety of income streams will be built into your wealth plan, with some of these streams continuing years into the future – along with some more traditional types of investments that people often consider when looking at retirement.

Modern retirement planning for my clients usually means looking at four key pillars, each with a slightly different purpose, but together pulling towards something sensible, adaptable and designed for the future that YOU are planning, which will be different to what I want. Or anyone else.

So, let's chat about the options available to you, and then we'll move on to how you can make sure that the money NEVER runs out (which I know is one of the main reasons you picked up this book). And we're also going to cover how you could create an income of more than £40,000 a year and pay no income tax whatsoever (without resorting to some dodgy tax avoidance scheme). How great is that?

Pensions & ISAs

I'm covering these two together because both are just different tax-wrappers that look to achieve a similar outcome, and typically contain the same contents in terms of investments. There are some exceptions to this (like defined benefit or final salary pensions) but on the whole, both pensions and ISAs are a mix of assets which you leave to grow until you need them.

Most pensions and ISAs contain what we call a collective investment.

These are funds that contain a wide range of shares, bonds, exposure to rental property etc., and effectively, you buy shares in the fund. The fund will either be actively managed, with a fund manager choosing what will be inside, or will be a passive index tracker. Index trackers follow the movement of a specific index (like the FTSE100), by buying shares in a range of popular companies (largely controlled by computer).

Both types of fund are available with different combinations of components, so you can take more or less risk with your money depending on your personal preference, and you can choose funds that are Ethically and Sustainability focused –

or even Sharia complaint funds. And once you've selected the fund that meets your risk appetite, you then need to decide how you are going to hold your investment – which means you need to choose a wrapper for your fund.

Although you can hold them in a simple investment account, this means you'll be paying more tax than you need to, either now or in years to come. So, most people either use a pension or ISA wrapper for their investments, but some business owners use a mixture of both to give them the best of both worlds because the tax treatment of each is very different.

A pension will give you tax relief on your contributions.

Every £100 you put in personally has £25 added free by HMRC (more if you're a higher rate tax payer). Your business can also pay into your pension as part of your benefits package and receive corporation tax relief on the money invested. If you invest the maximum £40,000, you'll save £7600 off your corporation tax bill that year... and you can do this each year.

BUT the downside of a pension investment is that you can't have the money until you're 55 or older (and anything that says otherwise is a scam!). You'll also be liable for tax on some of the money, when the time comes to take an income from it. The amount of tax you pay will depend on the other income you have at the time.

An ISA has no upfront tax relief but any money you take from it is tax-free in the future.

So, you can use an ISA to top-up your pension or earned income without paying any more tax.

You can also take this money out before you are 55 – although like all investments, because the market is volatile over the short-term, it's always advisable to leave the money for at least 5-10 years before you look to withdraw it. But this does mean it can play an important role as part of your flexible and adaptable plan, allowing you to work less hard much earlier than you thought possible by having money available to you in your 40s or early 50s.

And you know how the statutory wording goes – past performance is not a reliable indicator of future growth, and you may get out less than you put in.

But if you look at the past from 1925 to 2018, there is a general upwards trend over the long term.

So whichever way you go on this, pension, ISA, or both, the next step is to set up your regular monthly payment into your investment product.

As a quick aside, to get this level of growth on your ISA it needs to be investment based (what they used to call a stocks and shares ISA). A cash ISA offered by your bank is not going to give you this level of return. At time of writing, the best-buy cash ISAs were only offering 0.55-0.65% interest, which means if you paid in £10,000 after one year, they would pay you £55-65 interest. You could get up to 1.5% if you were prepared to tie up your money for 5 years, but that's still only

£150 interest, whereas in an investment ISA with a 7% rate of return, you'd have more than £4000 GROWTH over the same period.

THIS is why, when it comes for investing for the future, it's crucial that you start as early as you can! The sooner you start, the longer your money has to grow. If need be, start with a small amount – £100 or so – that you pay regularly every month. You'll start to build a pot of money which will grow all by itself. By investing monthly, you can take advantage of fluctuations in unit price – buying more units when the price is low, and fewer when prices are higher. Which over the long term, is more successful than trying to time the market and invest when prices are low. Like the old saying goes: It's not about timing the market, it's about time IN the market...

£100 a month invested in a fund growing at 7% a year – quite typical for an index tracker – is likely to get you around £123,000 in 30 years' time.

And if you invested £240 a month into a pension for your child until they were 18 – and then they continue paying in £180 a month – they could retire with a pot worth around a £1 MILLION.

It's to do with compounding and re-investing of dividends. Which means you can build quite a sizeable sum, over time. Now don't panic if your pension pot is empty, you're really not alone and there are still loads of options open to you!

It's often something that gets pushed to the back burner as we get on with growing our business, paying off our debts. And then we start to look at this bank account with money in and know it's time to start to do something with it.

To open a pension or Stocks and Share ISA, you can go online and use a reputable, self-managed platform. Or you can get help from a qualified financial adviser – like me! – to make 100% sure you have the right product, at the right risk level for your needs – please get in touch and chat about how we can get this moving for you (if you don't have a financial adviser that you're working with already).

Whichever path you choose, remember this is money you need to tie up for at LEAST 5 years.

This is long-term growth, not get rich quick.

Income from your business.

Income from your business can play a really important part of your future planning, especially if you have a source of passive income or a team that let you step back from the day-to-day arrangements whilst still allowing you to draw an income.

Passive income is about creating an asset once, which then pays you an ongoing income. It's always been popular in the music and film industry, where some artists literally live off the royalties that come in from their chart-topping or award-winning contribution. Some of those love-to-hate Christmas songs earn their artists and producers a multi-six figure sum

EVERY year from radio plays and streaming services, despite them not actively performing for years.

So, it's worth thinking about the assets you currently have, or are planning, and working out how best to structure your offering so that you can generate income from them now and in to the future. A couple of well written books or online programmes (if you're not up for creating a chart-topping musical hit) could allow you to create an income stream that will supplement any other income that you have, right the way through your retirement and beyond (The Bing Crosby foundation receives more than £120k a year for White Christmas and he's been dead since 1977).

The other way of having income from your business without actively working (or at least, keeping your input to a minimum) is to have a team of people who run the business for you. This might be your plan for your current business, where over time you'll bring in support staff and trained experts and so you'll work towards handing over the reins and only popping in for the staff Christmas meal.

Or you could look to buy or set up a completely different business in another industry. You don't need to be a plumber to run a plumbing and heating company, but you do need to understand all the rules and regulations, hire the right (qualified staff) plus some sort of business manager or COO (Chief Operating Officer) to run the business on your behalf. It's fair to say doing this in a completely new industry can be hard, so it's usually best to do something that you or your partner have some knowledge or familiarity with. But I've seen it work successfully with many of my clients.

The other part of your business income to look at is your client facing work. Is it likely that you'll still work with some of your clients but maybe be more choosy about which clients, and which of your services? Or will you look to step back from this side all together?

When making your Wealth Plan, it's usual to timeline out the income streams so that you can predict where your income will come from and what your expenses will look like. This is often referred to as cash flow modelling. You can do this on a piece of paper or use a spreadsheet or app to help you.

Doing this will mean you're clear on what money you will have available to you when, and mean that you can ensure that the money doesn't run out as long as you include a range of component parts.

So where does that £40k of income and no tax come in then?

The key here is maximising your tax allowances. We all have tax allowances. They may not sound glamourous or exciting, but very few people use them to their full extent (or even know what they are). Which truly is missing a trick, when it comes to planning and maximising your finances!

Here's how it works.

Every year, you don't have to pay tax on:

- £12,500 personal allowance, from your earned (or pension) income;
- £1,000 personal savings allowance (interest earned on your bank accounts);
- £2,000 dividends – like from a sale of shares, or drawn down from your business as part of your salary package;
- £12,300 Capital Gains Tax (CGT) – from the sale of your assets, like a rental/second property or antiques;
- £7,500 from renting a room, on the Government 'Rent a Room' Scheme;
- And £5,000 starter rate for savings (again from interest in bank accounts – but this does disappear as your earnings increase over £12,500).

Some or all of the tax allowances will apply to you. Once you understand what allowances are available and how best to use them, you can structure your income streams so that you're using as many allowances as possible.

So HOW do you get OVER the £40,000 I mentioned?

Well, this is where ISAs come into play!

There's common misconception that ISAs are complicated. Really, they're pretty straightforward.

An ISA is a savings or investment account, which you never pay tax on. With ISAs, you can save up to a maximum of £20,000 per year (for 2020/21), tax free, from April to April.

You can use any combination of the ISA types that you are eligible for (excluding the cash ISA – I've already explained why you'd want to avoid that one). So, for example, £14,000 in Innovative Finance ISA + £6,000 in a Stocks and Shares ISA (as long as your total tax-free ISA savings don't exceed £20,000 in any one tax year). The great thing is that ANY income earned from dividends from shares within your ISA is free of Income Tax with NO LIMIT, compared to the £2,000 dividend tax allowance if you held the shares outside the ISA wrapper.

There's also NO Capital Gains Tax to pay when you withdraw money from your ISA, even if it means you sell some shares for more than you bought them for. Shares held outside this protective wrapper are subject to CGT on profits over your £12,300 CGT allowance otherwise. So, by using your full ISA allowance and paying in £20,000 a year, you're effectively shielding this income from the tax man.

And when the time is right, you could pull out UNLIMITED money from your ISA with no further tax to pay – your ONLY limit is how much you've saved!

Reading this chapter hopefully means you've realised that you need a mixture of assets and income streams to ensure you're maximising your income, whilst minimise your tax as you go, and ensuring that at retirement, you've grown your asset pot in the most efficient way.

So, let's chat a bit more about the other components that you might look to include in your wealth plan and how each can help you with diversifying your investment risks.

Property.

I'm sure you own your own home, or are working towards buying a place of your own. It seems to be one of those things that we like to do. It gives us stability and security, and the ability to really make a house feel like a home, by having everything the way that you choose. Over time, the hope is that the value of the property will increase, you'll repay the mortgage, and be sitting on an asset of considerable value.

On top of this, lots of business owners consider buying some rental property so that they have another income stream plus a house that increases in value over time. This can be a great option for *some* people, for *some* of their money, but it's certainly not the holy grail that it was 10-20 years ago (contrary to what many property investment clubs will tell you).

Rental property can be regarded as a semi-passive income stream, once you've got some reliable tenants in place and, ideally, an experienced letting agent managing the property for you. But you'll still need to buy and sell property, arrange for maintenance and repairs and play your part in the tenant finding and letting process.

Most investors will buy a property with a deposit plus a buy-to-let mortgage, and depending on where you are in the UK, the amount of deposit that you need will vary. The amount you can borrow on a buy-to-let mortgage will depend primarily on the rental income of the property, your non-rental income and whether you are buying it as an individual or as a limited company. It's best to have an experienced financial adviser help you find the best mortgage for their circumstances, so that you can borrow what you need with the minimum of fuss. The fees they charge are deductible from your rental profit as a business expense, and their expertise will save you hours of time.

Sometimes you can buy a run-down property for cash, and then re-finance a few months later, after you've modernised and improved the property and it has increased in value. This may enable you to pull out most of the money you invested, but these deals are getting increasingly harder to find.

People like Robert Kiyosaki will argue that your own home doesn't count as an asset as you don't derive an income from it (unless you're renting out rooms or listing it on AirBnB when you go away), but in the financial planning world, your home is an asset – and often the biggest asset that you hold. But that doesn't mean that you can JUST own your home and a couple of rental properties and think that this is the end of your wealth plan.

Remember that catchy phrase from the last chapter? Your kids can't eat bricks. And neither can you. So, we're not going to want to put all of our money into one kind of asset. You're going to create a plan that brings together what you already have (old pensions/investments, rental property, business income) and fill the gaps to create a well-rounded and flexible plan.

The good news is that it's perfectly simple to create a plan that gives you plentiful income in your lifetime, plus a legacy for those that you leave behind. But the bad news is that this isn't going to happen on its own. It's going to take a few hours work now to create your plan, choose your mix of assets/income streams and then take action to implement what you've decided.

Creating this worry-free lifestyle that carries on into retirement might be THE thing on your vision board that you want to achieve most, and choose to focus your efforts on. Or it may only be a secondary consideration, that you know will benefit you over the short-term (in terms of tax relief) whilst also creating long-term wealth. But don't worry if you're not ready to tackle this yet, or have something else to cross off your list first.

That is ok. Do one thing at a time. But don't put it off too long, as the impact of delaying can be HUGE!

Easy for me to say, but to really get your head round the numbers, I thought I'd include a case study here so you can better see how future planning works.

The case study

Amy decided to start a pension 10 years ago and yet her retirement fund is empty.

Not because the stock market crashed, the pension company went bust or she was scammed, but because she only decided to start the pension. She didn't get as far as setting one up and paying in any money – which means she's potentially missed out on £422,000 growth on her retirement fund.

OMG!!

Most people's future plans will involve money in some way (either growing it, or paying down a mortgage), but if they don't actually take action, then in 10 years' time they'll be in the same place as now and they'll have to work even harder to achieve their goals as they'll have 10 years less time to get there.

So, let me tell you more about Amy. Not her real name obviously, confidentiality is key with all of my clients... but her story is typical of clients who come to work with me 1-2-1 to get support in building their wealth, often after they've confused themselves trying to go it alone and need someone to hold their hand to get it done.

Amy has a business turning over about £90,000 a year and is looking to end up with an income of £5000 a month when she chooses to work less hard in the future.

Like many entrepreneurs, she never really plans to stop working – more to become a bit more fussy about which projects she takes on - so she'll still look to draw an income of about £1000 a month from her business once she reduces her hours.

She'll also be entitled to a state pension of £760 a month from age 68, earned from the National Insurance contributions that she (and her business) have paid in over the years.

So she's going to need an additional £3240 a month to reach her £5000 a month target.

With me so far?

That's about £39,000 a year, but for how many years?

Now, I don't have a crystal ball, but the average life expectancy for someone in their 30s is 94 years old, so we're going to need to look at a pot of about £1 million if Amy wants consistent income for the whole of her retirement. Sounds like a lot of money – and it is, but it's perfectly achievable for a business owner at or around the 6-figure mark.

In practice, she won't need nearly as much as this in her pension pot, for three main reasons:

1. Most people spend more in their 50s and 60s than they do in their 70s and 80s, so it's likely that she could comfortably live on an income of about £2500 a month from age 75.
2. Throughout her retirement, her pot will continue to

grow as she'll only take out what she needs and leave
the rest invested

3. She's likely to have income from other sources – she
   may downsize her home, or sell her business as a
   going concern, both of which will release money that
   she could use to top up her income.

So, let's say she needs £39000 for the first seven years of her
retirement, plus £9000 a year in the remaining 19 years. That
means she'll need a minimum pot of around £444,000 –
although obviously it would be great to have more.

To achieve a pot of that size, her £400 a month contribution
needs to grow at a rate of about 6.5% after fees and charges
over the next 30 years – which is quite feasible in an 'average'
fund.

But the bad news....

If she'd started 10 years ago then at retirement her pot would
be more than double this – at a little over £900,000. By not
paying in over the last 10 years, as well as the £48000 she's
not paid in contributions she's missed out on the compounded
effect of the growth of the money.

There's a phenomenon in investing called the rule of 72 – a
simplified way to work out how quickly your money grows –
and the result of this is that at a 7% growth rate, your money
will double every 10 years.

And at a 10% growth rate, your money doubles every 7 years.

Which means for Amy, her pot of £442k could have been £913k.... oops!

But what can she do now if she wants to ensure that she ends up nearer to her 'nice to have' figure of £1 million? (Given that going back in time 10 years to start payments in isn't an option) ...

There are two main choices:

1) She could invest more money per month – she'd need to increase the £400 per month to £830 per month to get to the same end point.

Missing out on those 10 years of contributions, and the compounded growth means that ideally, she needs to double the amount she pays in, but if this isn't feasible for her budget, then even a small increase can make a massive difference.

It's worth remembering that your Ltd. company can pay into your director's pension (providing you have the set up the right type of scheme) and so you could use this to direct surplus profits to your pension from your company account before your accountant completes your year end. This has the knock-on effect of reducing your corporation tax bill, which means that you may end up with spare money in your tax savings account at the end of the year – hooray!

2) She could find a fund that is growing at 10% a year – so opting for something with a slightly greater level of risk than she originally planned

I'm not talking about investing in unlisted companies, bitcoin or anything unusual – simply choosing a pension or investment fund that is one risk level higher than she would normally. So maybe choosing moderate rather than cautious, or active growth instead of moderate (or however your pension provider categorises them – some use a number scale from 1-7).

Otherwise, she may need to accept that some of her retirement income will need to come from other sources, like her business or a rental property, or from downsizing her home.

But there's a REALLY big elephant in the room here – What about the tax?

Remember that all income from a pension that falls over the personal tax-free allowance will be taxed (at 20% or 40%) and so to get an income of £60,000 a year, Amy will need to draw out £79,200 from her pension so that after the tax has been paid, she still gets the monthly sum she needs. (Based on the current tax thresholds – these tend to rise each year, but we can't predict what these allowances will be at retirement).

She could reduce this tax liability considerably (or even to zero) by putting some of her monthly contributions into an ISA rather than a pension - remember there is no tax payable on money when it comes out of an ISA. So, if her £60k a year was made up of £12500 pension plus £47,500 from her ISA, she'd pay no income tax at all, and not need a pot that was quite as large as if it were all in a pension. But you can only pay into an ISA from your personal savings, and not from your business, so it will depend where her excess income currently sits.

Working out how big a pot you'll need for a very comfortable and active retirement (and how much you need to put away each month to get there) is part of the Wealth Plan that I help my clients create as part of my six-month Wealth Builder Experience, or in my signature programme, Magnetic Wealth ™ in our 1-2-1 sessions. We'll also look at how to hold the various components to maximise growth and minimise tax now, and when you come to draw on the money in the future.

But if you'd like to make a start on your own, you can find some great resources to help you at our online support page. Find out more about how to get access to this in chapter 9.

Ok, so we've covered the types of things to include in your wealth plan, and how to stop the money running out – the next chapter will cover the step which is almost as important as creating your wealth plan. The step which people success-fully growing their assets feel is fundamental to their success... (and it doesn't even have to cost any money)...

Let's move on -->>

8

WHAT'S IN YOUR DRAWER?? - REVIEW
AND TWEAK

~ A Story ~

When I bought my first home in 1999, like many people I went for an interest-only mortgage plus a with-profits endowment plan. This seemed like the most amazing way to repay my mortgage AND get a cash lump sum in 25 years' time which I could use to go on holiday or create a nest egg with. Plus, I got FREE life cover to repay the mortgage – what could possibly go wrong?

That's what the 'mortgage adviser' in the estate agent told me at the time (for reasons that became apparent much further down the line, which I'll go into shortly). And as a 20-something with no financial knowledge, and in the days before the internet, I went along with what he said.

I'm sure you've heard about endowments – those nightmare investment policies that so many people bought in the 1980s and 1990s, except that at the time, we didn't know what a headache they would prove to be later down the line.

The mortgage salesman (prior to 2002, you didn't need any formal qualifications to be a mortgage adviser) had a glossy and compelling brochure that showed how this amazing product would provide a lump sum on top of repaying my mortgage and how much better this would be than taking out a repayment mortgage.

I'm sure if I'd looked at the brochure in detail (and known what to look for in the small print) I'd have realised that:

1. There were no guarantees that it would repay my mortgage;
2. He got a massive commission to sell me the product;
3. His fee, plus all the other charges taken over the first few years, meant that the pot wasn't worth what I'd paid in to it if I surrendered it early.

Luckily, I only kept mine for less than 2 years, and when I next moved house opted for a much safer repayment mortgage. I only got a refund of about £300 on my endowment, but I was glad to draw a line under it and learn a lesson. Many people were not so fortunate.

The biggest problem with endowments wasn't that they were poorly performing investments with a whole load of cloaked and hidden charges.

It was that people bought them with a view to using it to pay off their mortgage, and put it in a drawer and ignored it for 20 years, only pulling it out when they started to realise that their mortgage lender would soon be looking for repayment of the lump that was owed.

Which is why I'm including this example in a chapter about reviewing your finances on a regular basis, in case you wondered where this story was headed...

The letters that came in the post from the insurance company telling them that the endowment wasn't performing as expected and that they were predicted to have a shortfall when it came to the time to repay their mortgage, usually got put in the drawer with an "I'll deal with it later" attitude. Except most of them didn't deal with it until it was much too late, and then they had few options available to them.

This meant hundreds of thousands of borrowers were left with no way to repay their interest only mortgage, because their endowment hadn't performed as they originally expected. A lot of them ended up getting squeezed onto repayment mortgages with only a few years to go until they retired. This meant they ended up with massive monthly mortgage repayments just so they could get their mortgage repaid before their main income stopped. Others had to sell up and move away from the house that they loved, and buy somewhere else smaller (that didn't need a mortgage), away from their friends and family.

Neither of which was the outcome they thought they were getting when they signed on the dotted line.

Putting the right things in place to build an amazing future for you and your family is an EPIC thing, but you need to make sure that you're checking in on them regularly so that you know that they are doing what they are meant to be doing. And that they are still helping you move towards that future you want.

Leaving them sat in the drawer for years on end, thinking that it's one-and-done, can mean that you have a massive gap when you need it most.

You'll be pleased to hear that the sale of financial services products has changed a lot in the last few years, which means that as a consumer, you get a lot more protection and are largely protected from the horror stories of the past. Rules and regulations have been tightened progressively over the last 20 years and it means that the new world of financial advice looks much different from when I took out my first mortgage in 1999.

The biggest overhaul happened in 2012 with a thing called RDR.

The Retail Distribution Review (RDR) brought into line some things that you would have thought would be commonplace in the financial services world, but were in fact completely alien. Like your financial adviser having any recognised qualifications in finance.

Prior to this date, it seems that all and sundry would be selling insurance products or pensions, and acting like glorified sales-people, with no training, no qualifications, and ultimately, for the consumer, no fall-back if anything went wrong. From RDR, it became mandatory to have an approved level four (degree level) qualification in finance to be able to call yourself a financial adviser, which led to a huge increase in the number of 'advisers' retiring or leaving the profession.

The other big thing that changed at this point was that the rules changed in terms of what happened with fees and charges and how you pay for the financial advice you receive.

Financial Services is something that you pay for, you've always paid for it. The difference is that these days, you know how much you're going to pay, to whom and when. It's all done in a way that is transparent and fair, which works so much better with how I like to run my business. I never would have wanted to be involved with the way things were done in the old days pre-RDR.

In previous days, many people thought that financial advice was free, because the person that sold them their pension, endowment or mortgage didn't ask them for any money or provide an invoice. If they'd dug deeply into the reams of paperwork they'd been provided with (remember how many trees we cut down before PDFs became commonplace...) they may have found some information about fees, but let's face it, who actually reads the small print? It's like those websites you go on that say *tick here to say you've read terms and conditions* when in fact, most people take it to mean *tick here to move on to the next page.*

So many people didn't understand that the advice they thought they were getting for free actually involved a whole load of hidden fees and charges within the financial products they were paying for. They thought that setting their pension up was free, or they saw the setting their endowment up was free and didn't realise that for the first two or three years, a huge proportion of the premiums they were paying were going towards commissions and kickbacks for all sorts of salespeople along the chain. This meant that if they decided to cash in their plan early, they often got back less than they'd paid into it. Not great.

And there was no incentive for the 'adviser' to have any further contact with the clients once the product had been set up. They'd been paid and would move on to the next sale – where the size of the commission they were being offered would often affect which provider they chose to recommend to their clients.

RDR meant a complete overhaul of how financial advisers typically run their businesses and charge their clients for the work they do and the advice they provide. Most of us now choose to take a small fee from our clients upfront and then charge a smaller ongoing fee to cover those important regular review meetings and all the ongoing advice that ensures that things are on track for the goals and objectives that have been set.

Other financial advisers charge a fee upfront for set up, and then invoice separately for follow up meetings but either way, the hidden fees are a thing of the past! And most clients are seen at least once a year to review suitability and get advice from a qualified professional, Hooray!

(And if you want to check that your adviser is qualified, you can look on the FCA register online to find out.)

If you choose to set up your own financial products, then you need to make sure that you're taking the time to regularly check they still meet your needs, and from time to time, seek alternative options so that you don't get any nasty shocks further down the road. The internet makes this easier than in days gone past, but you'll still need to scrutinize the small print. It may be possible to get support from a financial adviser as a one-off to check you're understanding the paperwork you have correctly.

But it's not only your financial products that need a regular check-up – you also need to ensure that you're hitting the milestones and markers that you've set on that incredible plan that you've created. And that you're keeping your everyday finances in good order, so that you don't get any nasty surprises at the end of the month when the money's not in the right place.

But which of these should you tackle first, and how often should you look at them?

I'm going to suggest there are three sets of things that you should be looking at, some of which are monthly, some of which are quarterly, and some you can get away with looking at once a year. And then I'm going to give you a few ideas as to how you can find a way to do this regularly that works for you.

So, let's talk about what those things are.

Things to look at monthly.

1) Assets and liabilities (Net Worth)

This means looking at the value of money in all your bank accounts, savings, investments, pensions, and also at how much money you owe people - your mortgage, loans, credit cards, that type of thing.

This enables you to calculate your Net Worth. Simply put, when you add up all the money (or all the assets) that you have and take off what you owe to everybody, your net worth is the figure that comes out the bottom.

By tracking this monthly, you should be able to see that your net worth is increasing over time, which is great as it is one measure of your financial strength. The amount of growth, month on month, will vary, but as you continue to pay into your savings and investments, and you pay down your mortgages and loans, you should find that your Net Worth increases over time.

There are lots of ways you can keep a record of this. The old school way is to write it down in an exercise book, and for some people this works really well. I use an Excel spreadsheet, which makes things much simpler (as it does the calculations for me and keeps things much more tidy than I could do with **my** handwriting).

It's a really simple spreadsheet which across the top has the months of the year, and then down the side, has a list of the things that I have as assets. Home, Pension, ISA, other investments, and each of my six bank accounts (from chapter 5).

Then I have a row for total assets – which I've used the excel autosum option to add up all the rows above (A).

Next, I have similar rows for the things that I have as debts, with a similar total (B).

And at the bottom, I have a figure for my Net Worth, which is (A) – (B).

It's quite easy to set up a sum of one minus the other if you're quite crafty with an Excel spreadsheet. And if you're not sure how, there are many tutorials on YouTube or Google, or check out chapter 9 if you want a FREE copy of the one I use, with the formatting included.

If you know that a spreadsheet isn't a good option for you, or haven't got time to set one up, then please use an exercise book to create a similar table so that you can start your review process NOW, rather than adding this to your one-day-I'll do-it-list. You (or your assistant) can always transfer the numbers over to a spreadsheet later.

Remember, this is a snapshot of your financial position, so it's best to use the same sources of data and ideally do it on the same day each month. I do mine on the first Monday of each month, but you can choose a date that works best in your dairy.

It's easy enough to log in to your internet banking apps and get up to date balances on most things, although you may need to call your mortgage lender if they don't have an online facility to get your current balance.

When it comes to the number to put in for the property value of the home that you live in, there's lots of ways that you can do this. You could look at getting your house professionally valued once a year and use this figure for the whole year, or so you could look at a local house price index. Personally, I tend to use Zoopla where you can put your postcode in and, using the house prices feature, it will tell you what it thinks the current value is, based on when your house was purchased. It gives a range of values. I tend to use the lower one because I like to be optimistically cautious. And then I know my assets are worth at least this and I keep an eye on it, see what it does over time.

2) Profit in your business

The other thing you should be checking monthly is the profit levels within your business. In the online world, it seems that everybody is very focused on how much money your business makes in terms of sales. But ultimately, making sales is not as important as the PROFIT that your business is making.

Why? Because the profit is the money that you are going to use to pay your own personal income each month!!

You can calculate your profit by using your online accounting software (Xero/QuickBooks etc.) or by looking at figures for money incoming to your Stripe/PayPal accounts and deducting an estimate of this month's costs. Do it in whichever way works for you, but do have a look at it (rather than wait for your accountant to tell you at the end of the year).

You should find that as your turnover increases, your profit also increases – although often by a smaller amount as it costs more to run a bigger business (you can't do it all on your own) – but it should be increasing overall.

Things to look at Quarterly

Your quarterly review is designed to look at the medium-term trends within your personal and business finances and to keep on top of things that will need dealing within the next year.

Take a look at your **personal accounts.** Are you putting the right percentage of your drawings in each, or do you regularly need to borrow from other pots? Remember that it will take some time for things to stabilize (up to 18 months) as some larger expenses are only paid annually, but on the whole, each account should have a reasonable balance and not be empty the day before your standing order arrives.

Your business accounts should all have money in them (except maybe your incoming money account if you've moved all your money out to the other accounts in the last few days).

If you have a large surplus in your **owners pay account** (more than 3-6 months drawings) consider whether you'd like to pay yourself a little more each month and/or increase the amount your business pays into your pension. Only increase the payment(s) slightly – by £200-£500 a month, and then take another look next quarter to see if it is sustainable to increase again. It's much better to be consistent than to have to put it down again later.

If you've regularly had to borrow money from your owner's pay or tax account to pay your expenses, you may need to increase the amount you leave in the operating expenses account (and reduce your own pay) or find other ways to reduce expenses in your business. Take a look through the things on your bank statement to see if there are any things that you no longer need, subscriptions from groups you don't attend or if there is a more cost-effective way to pay for your phone and internet.

End dates on any 0% credit cards or fixed term investment plans

If you've got a balance on a credit card that you're repaying, double check when the end date of the 0% period is and work out if you will have cleared it in full before the hefty interest rate kicks in when the rate expires. You may need to increase your monthly payments to get it repaid, or make plans to transfer it to another 0% deal before the interest starts. Looking at these regularly will avoid you getting caught out, and give you plenty of time to sort out a new card (if you don't have an existing card to transfer it to).

Now that you have a pot of money for emergencies, you shouldn't need to be using this credit card at all and should aim to pay it off in a way that works with your surplus income each month – be mindful that each time you move it to another card you'll be charged a fee.

If you have a savings account or cash ISA with an introductory rate, you need to be aware of when the bonus period ends so that you can move your money to another account as soon as your rate drops.

Your big plan – are you moving forward? What are you goals for the next quarter?

We've spoken in earlier chapters about getting clear picture of your dream and creating a plan to make it happen. So, that thing that you've decided that you want and have now mapped out to create, you're going to need to keep on top of it and make sure that you're actually making progress towards it.

You've heard me talk about tweak and review, and that's all it needs to be. Every so often, just make those little changes to ensure that everything is on track for that thing you're aiming for. You don't need to keep re-writing your plan, simply check in on where you are and make sure you have some actions for the next few months.

The reason that milestones and markers are so important is that we often need to adjust our expectations or timescales, because life throws things at us or our circumstances change.

Say you're trying to save up for an amazing round the world trip that is £20,000 pounds, which you plan to take in five years' time. You set up your initial payment to go in at £100 pound a month to a savings account, with a view to increasing the amount you pay in when your car finance ends/you start to draw more from your business/Christmas is out of the way. How disappointed are you going to be if you don't actually look at that bank account for five years, and then, when you do look at it realise there's not as much money in there as you hoped and you need to postpone your trip (or book cheaper hotels and flights and lose out on the luxury vibe you were aiming for)?

You need to be able to make sure that at regular intervals, you're looking to see what the balances in your accounts are. What the balance of your mortgage is if you're aiming to repay it. Or how much you've grown in your savings or your pensions or your investments, so that you can work out if you're actually on track to the goals you want. It might be that you're ahead of schedule, on track or behind, but by making time to look at it regularly, at least you'll know!!

When you look at the performance of your investments, if the performance is better than you expected, you might find you don't need to add in quite so much money each month, which means you could divert that to something else. Looking at it the other way, if it hasn't performed as expected, like those endowments of the 1980s, you might need to put in more money, or change plans completely, so that you've got another way to meet the objective you want.

But putting your head in the sand like that ostrich back in chapter two is not the answer, you need to find a way to keep on top of it. Carving out a regular slot in your diary to look at your finances and your plan is one way to make sure that it gets done, rather than ending up in that *I'll do it one day* space (and then needing to deal with it last minute, when you hit a crisis point).

Things to look at Annually

Here's the time to take an overall look at Your big plan, Your Net Worth and Your business turnover/profit for the year. Have you made the progress you wanted? And if not, what do you need to do differently NEXT year? Is there something you want to add to your vision board/plan for next year, or want to remove as your priorities have changed?

Look back at your figures for the year compared to the previous year so that you can be proud of what you've achieved and take some time to celebrate your success. We often get so caught up in the things we didn't do, that we don't appreciate how far we've come! It's possible that this year you've earned more per month than you did per year in the corporate world, or that you've finally become debt-free. Celebrate your success – you're doing great!

Take time to do some basic financial housekeeping, looking at things like **your mortgage** – when does the current fixed-rate deal end? Do you need to make contact with your financial adviser to chat about options and next steps, or submit your accounts soon to ensure that they're ready for your mortgage application? Do you need to liaise with your financial adviser and accountant about the number of dividends you should declare this year to ensure that you can borrow the amount that you need, whilst minimising your personal tax liability?

Take a quick glance over your **protection plans and Will** – has anything changed in your circumstances which means that you might need to review the arrangements that you have made? Are you now a Ltd. company (which can pay into your pension and provide death in service for you as an employee), or have you separated/divorced/retired your husband (and are now reliant on only your income), or increased the size of your family?

Put a date in your diary for the renewals of your **Home insurance, car insurance and breakdown cover** – you can save hundreds of pounds a year by not allowing it to auto-renew, and put this money you save towards something else on your vision board!

Take this opportunity to do your financial filing, scanning important documents and shredding the paper copies to keep everything accessible and to ensure that you've prepared a file with where to find all your important financial information, should your family ever need to access things on your behalf.

What this regular review process ultimately achieves

If you'd asked me when I set out to write this book the main advantage that regularly checking in on your finances has, I'd have to say confidence that you're on track, and a better understanding of your money so that you can confidently chat to your accountant, colleagues and staff members about money.

But that misses a really important part.

The EXCITEMENT that you feel seeing your balances increase, KNOWING that you're making progress towards your goals whilst enjoying an incredible standard of living – Without WORRY that the money will run out.

Regular money check-in sessions means you can keep an eye on the systems that you've set up, and have the ability to spot any problems whilst they're still relatively small (rather than one day finding the money all gone).

If you realise that quarterly, your savings are depleting as you regularly use them to prop up your spending, it gives you time to work on earning more or spending less and means that you avoid that omg – panic - moment!!!

As you see the surplus in your business account building, it gives you time to make your partner or adult children shareholders to extract some extra tax-free dividends before the end of the tax year, or to increase salaries and pension contributions for you and your staff, to reduce your corporation tax bill.

And like the barometer on the side of the church hall, watching the balance increase in your dream fund grow, month-on-month, spurs you on to take more aligned action to make things happen. Like the buzz you get when a Stripe payment pings or a client signs up to your programme, hitting your savings thresholds feels INCREDIBLE!

Getting your finances in order and really understanding how your money works will have a massive impact on how you feel about life. Leaving you free to get on with living the life you love, whatever that looks like for you.

No guilt over how you spend your money and a sense of calm and confidence knowing that you have things in place so that the money doesn't run out.

But this isn't all about you. It's about the legacy that you leave for the future.

Being able to confidently chat about money with the children in your world means you can create a lasting impact that benefits generations to come. You can help them write their own positive money stories, create their own simplified wealth plans and by following your example, they will realise that making good money allows them to have an impact in the world, and this is something to be proud of.

I know this all sounds amazing, but how can you make sure that you make time to do this, and that your plan doesn't sit in a drawer, unactioned for the next 20 years...?

Let's go on to the final chapter to find out...

9

WHAT'S NEXT?

So here we are. You now know what you need to do.

But are you actually going to do it? Or will this book end up on the shelf with The Richest Man in Babylon, Chillpreneur and the others that you promised yourself would be the solution?

Only you can decide. But there are ways that I can help you, if now is the right time for you to take action on this.

Let's take a moment to consider some alternatives here...

Going out and making more money is certainly one of them. There are lots of coaching programmes and masterminds that promise to 10x your income – and you could probably still squeeze a few extra hours out of your working week, right?

But you've already done that, haven't you? You thought that (with a bit of sweaty grind) you'd hit that 6-figure income, and finally have enough money to start investing properly and living the life that you love. Yet here you are, growing your income while your wealth is being eroded. Inflation is literally eating away at the value of your hard-earned money as it sits in your savings account doing nothing!!

And instead of doubling your wealth every six to nine years, you're likely trading entire luxury holidays for inflated tax bills every year and don't feel any more wealthy than you did three years ago (despite making much more money). And you're certainly not moving towards your dreams as quick as you'd like.

There really are only two options here:

Focus on making more money or focus on building more wealth.

So let me chat you through HOW I can help you move forward, and then tell you about WHERE you can find all those juicy extra resources I've mentioned throughout the book.

Ways to work with me.

ROCK Solid ™

This book gives an overview of the ROCK Solid™ method that I use with all my clients, but if you'd like a structured way to get those things accomplished, then the six-week supported study programme is the first step. You can access this from www.peacetogether.co.uk and if you use the code ROCK500 at the checkout, you'll get discounted access as a thank you for reading my book.

It's totally self-study, so you can work at home and in private, without sharing *any* of your financial information with anyone, all on an online platform. You can fit it in before your working day starts, if that's what works for you, or do some bite-sized learning while you sit waiting in the car at the school gates.

We're going to deal with those things that are crucial to business owners, to give you that peace of mind with your money. The stuff you *know* you need to do, but never quite get around to! But that make a MASSIVE difference.

You'll work on your financial foundations that form the 'ROCK' in ROCK Solid™:

R = Regular Income

O = Organise Your Finances

C = Comfort Blanket: Your Financial Safety Net

K = Know Your Focus + Your Plan!

Once you've worked through the material, there are a range of accountability and support programmes available to you depending on your situation and the amount of further support you need including:

From time to time, I run ROCK Solid ™ as a LIVE in-person programme, so that those who would rather blast through in a couple of days can just get it done in one go. Contact us to ask about dates, or keep an eye on our social media.

The Asset Accelerator

Is a way for me to take the plan you've created and support you to take the action needed to move forward with the re-assurance of quarterly 1-2-1 meetings to look at their financials and tweak their plan.

It is open to business owners and employees at all stages of their financial journey, who need to hold a monthly space to take action. A no-frills option, which runs on a monthly basis with no ongoing tie in, providing huge value at an affordable monthly cost.

Magnetic Wealth ™

This is my signature VIP 1-2-1 programme for female business owners making at, or above, £85-200k per year and it is incredible! This exclusive, application only container supports 10 hand-picked women in growing their personal estate to multi-six figures within 3-5 years.

In 14 years of working with female business owners, I've heard it many times:

"I'm too busy making sales to stop and work out what I'm meant to be doing with the money I'm making."

They feel like they're not doing all the grown-up things they should do. They're anxious that their amazing business could come crashing down around them at any point, ultimately devastating their family. They tell me that they love group experiences (with the right people), but would never want to share any of their personal wealth information with other participants.

And they say they love working 1-2-1 with me as an expert because of the simple way that I explain complicated concepts... that I'm "fun and approachable".

Connection with confidentiality. Personal attention from a professional with a splash of personality.

There was nothing like this out there in the market place. Something was Missing... So, I Created It.

I decided to offer the best of both worlds in one ...*and Magnetic Wealth^{TM}* was born.

Get private wealth-creation guidance, while being supported by other high-vibe entrepreneurs.

This is a completely new experience.

Not a group coaching programme.

Not a mastermind.

It's **a twelve-month transformative wealth experience** that will forever alter how you deal with your money, shifting you from dreaming of wealth to building it. Exactly like you've read about in this book.

Essentially, it's a 1-2-1 programme with me, plus input from an incredible money mindset coach and the most helpful accountant you could hope to meet.

And then we add in **online expert wealth seminars**, **2x in-person Woman of Wealth training days,** full access to **ROCK Solid™** and a host of other goodies that help you move from a money-making woman into truly being a wealthy woman.

Plus, you get a seat at our Interactive Monthly Implementation Sessions where you can hold the space in your diary to take action on your plan, whilst maintaining your privacy.

And you'll Be Part of an Exclusive Wealth-Building Community.

You'll get to share your journey with an intimate, carefully curated group of business owners, who will cheer you on and share encouragement - with zero judgment.

Deeply connect and share ideas with the best business buddies you never knew you had, in a Voxer/ WhatsApp community group - and also in person, at our in-person wealth events.

It truly is the most exciting, ground-breaking thing I've ever been part of!

Find out more at https://peacetogether.co.uk/magnetic-wealth/ or message me to see if this could be a good fit for you ☺

Okay, I'm interested in working with you. Is there a guarantee?

In life...? That you'll meet your soulmate? That your business will be a success?

Let me get my crystal ball, it's in the other bag...

If we're honest, there are very few guarantees in life.

But I can assure you that **if you join me with an open mind + take small amounts of regular action**... You will make massive progress towards growing your wealth.

You will also free up your time. You'll see your wealth grow.

You'll feel your financial confidence grow as you evolve within a business that serves you, rather than the other way around.

I can guarantee that I'll hold your hand and be a call away throughout our time together to answer your questions if you're my 1-2-1 client.

And that if you're in a programme without a 1-2-1 component, you'll have all the resources that you need to understand your options and take actions that move you forward.

I can guarantee that I will work through your own solutions, and not force my agenda on you.

I can guarantee that I will connect you to the top-notch experts that I have on speed dial (from Monday to Thursday).

(Yes, I can also guarantee that I don't work on Fridays).

Oh, I can offer you one more guarantee:

I guarantee that if you don't jump on this opportunity to turn your money into wealth...

You will have passed up on opportunities that can act as a powerful wealth accelerator and amplifier for you.

You will watch others taking hold of the life you desire.

You will continue to dream about being wealthy and living life your way.

Stop dreaming of wealth, and start building it. Let's go!

Regulated Financial Planning advice

After reading through this book, you may realise that you need help with arranging your financial planning and if you don't already have a financial adviser you can ask us to help you get the things in place that best meet your individual needs.

Our sister company, Claire at Blueprint, completes all our Regulated Advice and can help arrange (or consolidate) your pension, set up investments such as ISAs (or things for your children) and can arrange the mortgage for your dream (or next) home, to help you get in with as little fuss as possible.

We can also offer a one-stop shop when it comes to pulling together the parts that make up your Comfort blanket – we offer a **FREE protection review service where** we can look at what you have in place already and can look to set up new plans if needed. We can tailor the cover to your needs, so that you don't pay more than necessary and ensure you have the peace of mind you need.

We will also be able to put plans in trust so that they are not liable to inheritance tax (IHT) and can be paid quickly in event of a death - none of this needs to be complicated or scary, and we're going to talk you through all of it in simple, jargon-free language! (As you'd expect...)

Will-writing is done in partnership with a local Licenced Will-Writing firm who can provide our clients with Single or Mirror Wills so that their wishes are carried out after their death at a cost-effective rate, and from the comfort of your own home.

To start the process with any of your regulated financial planning needs or to chat to us about arranging an initial meeting, please to book an introductory call by phone on (01227) 283186 or by sending an email to ourpa@blueprintkent.co.uk

KEEPING IN TOUCH

I'm a people person, and love to chat to people (maybe a bit more than I should, but hey...) and I'd love to connect with you online, so that I can quietly smile to myself when I see you move forward in making your dream happen, and be there to publicly congratulate you with your successes.

It will also give you access to the raft of free, high-value content I post online every week.

Feel free to friend request me on Facebook – it's where I spend most of my time (just ask my husband).

You're welcome to check out my incredible Facebook group *It's THE Place to be* if you're looking for a positive, fun place to hang out online.

You'll also find me over on Instagram, and my YouTube channel has a great selection of easy to action videos, designed specifically for business owners

https://bit.ly/ClaireSweetYouTube

www.Instagram.com/peacetogethermoneycoach

If you'd like to send me a message to say what you thought of the book, or to ask about the best way for us to work together feel free – you can do that on Messenger here >>

https://m.me/ClaireSweet01

THOSE EPIC RESOURCES I MENTIONED

Head over to; https://book.peacetogether.co.uk/have-life-your-way/resources or scan the QR code to get FREE access to the budget planner, asset tracker, summary guide to Profit first and some other amazing tools I want to share with you to help you move forward in your financial journey.

 I ask that you keep these for your personal use, and that if you feel they would be useful to people that you know, that you connect us (or buy them a copy of this book) so that they can move forward in their journey at their own pace.

If you'd like to get a copy of When Women Heal and hear a little more about my story, you can buy a copy HERE >>

http://bit.ly/WhenWomenHeal

WHAT PEOPLE SAY

You'll have probably gathered by this part of my book, that I'm not overly bothered by what people think of me. I know that I'm amazing at what I do and that my work changes lives, and that I can help you create the life you love.

But I get that sometimes it's nice to hear what other people think too... especially if you've never heard of me before picking up this book!

So here are some comments from existing and previous clients, and people who I've had a positive impact on over the years. Feel free to look them up online if you want to chat more to them about me.

"Claire helped me to structure my business finances so I could pay myself a set amount each month and always have the money ready for my expenses, even when income is variable. This has allowed me to pay myself the same amount each month, even though I now take a whole month off each summer to go travelling in our motorhome with my family!

This was always the dream, but I never knew how to achieve it. Working with Claire has made that happen, even during a year where my turnover was hit by the pandemic. Last year was a month in Scotland, next up is a month touring France! I can now do this with confidence that a month out my business is manageable.

Sorting my business finances has now meant I am also contributing monthly to my pension. And in personal finances, for the first time ever, we are looking forward to Christmas without having to worry at all about paying for it as the money is already there. And we are also able to drip feed into investments.

Feeling this in control of our finances has been liberating. We know we are making steps towards our future dreams, whilst managing to meet our current obligations. I really wish we had met Claire years ago - so much stress would have been avoided and we would be even closer to our dreams already! But better late than never and at least now I know our dreams are achievable."

Marianne Killick
Integrative Women's Health coach and Author

"I have been in the financial services industry since we were 'policy peddlers', in an un-regulated free-for-all in the early

80s. In forty years, I could count on one hand the people that have truly impressed me. Claire is one of them.

When I first met Claire in 2012, it was evident that she was different, and would stand out not just for being a lady in a (then) man's world, but because she was intent on building a business based upon ethical behaviour, diligent effort, and making a difference.

I did not hesitate to embrace her, and she has astounded even me with her journey. Claire is the financial adviser I would have if I was not one myself...."

Ian Meekins
CEO Blueprint Financial Services

"When I was unhappy in my job and thinking of changing career, what worried me was how I would cope with potentially a major drop in income and thereby imposing a drastic change of lifestyle on my family.

I have known Claire since our children were very small; my husband and I were clients of hers from an early stage and she had already arranged several mortgages for us. Inspired by seeing Claire going for her own dream job, I talked to her about the practicalities of a career change. She talked me through the possibilities and financial implications, and showed me that what seemed like a major change in salary on the surface was, in fact, perfectly manageable, and not the scary prospect I had imagined it to be. From there, a move to a different career involving going back to University and retraining, went from being a pipe dream to a possibility and then to a reality.

Three years later, I have my dream job; I am crazy busy, but loving it! As for my family's lifestyle, we are still living in the same house, with no perceptible reduction in our standard of living. The difference is that I am no longer bored and frustrated in my work, but rather, I have a career now that I wholeheartedly believe in – it has made the most amazing difference to me and my family. I am so grateful for the honest and practical advice and support I got from Claire which kick-started my career change and made the seemingly impossible, possible."

Jayne H
Teacher, Friend and Client

"I have known Claire for many years. We met as I too am a financial planner and invariably in these circles, you meet up at various events. The first time we met, Claire was only working part time in financial services and you could see her passion - I implored her to go full time as she needed to commit to what she really believed in.

We have a lot in common (I don't have Alpacas though), in that we both genuinely LOVE to help clients to reach what their true potential really is, and often that means not just financial advice but coaching too. I know no one who does this better than Claire, but in two distinct ways. You see, unlike many "advisers" out there who don't practice what they preach, Claire does, and in doing so, has achieved many of her goals and wants to share, encourage and show you how to do the same, while speaking from the heart with conviction and empathy. Claire is totally unique in her approach, taking an often stuffy and unspoken subject of money, often associated with "men in suits" (her words!), and made money advice and guidance accessible to all for their true potential to be reached.

Claire has also guested on my BBC Radio show on numerous occasions, because of her ability to put complex matters into plain English, which is easy to do when you walk the walk. Claire is completely genuine – what you see isn't the usual bluster and show; it's the real deal – her true self. I admire Claire for just not what she has achieved, but where she is heading and her mission of helping others along a journey to similar happiness. It's financial planning – done right."

David Braithwaite
CEO Citrus Financial Management,
BBC Presenter and Conference Speaker

"Having connected with Claire in a couple of mutual groups online, I started following her for the interesting and really useful financial knowledge she shares. I then decided to work with Claire in person on one of her VIP days, as I knew I would learn a lot about finances - both in terms of personal and business finances.

The day was great and exceeded my expectations - not only did I finally get around to completing my Will, but was also able to map out and plan the next stages for my second property. Something I've wanted to do for a while, but didn't have all the knowledge and expertise Claire could offer.

During our 121 meeting, Claire was super helpful, non-judgemental (my previous history of student debts and credit cards didn't faze her), friendly and honest.

I learnt things that will serve me for life and was able to visualise a clear picture of where to go and what to do going forward. This clarity alone was worth the investment and I trust Claire to advise of the best options.

I have no doubt I will continue to work with Claire to help me on my financial journey.

As an added bonus, I also met her lovely family and the adorable alpacas."

Leanne Naylor
Sleep consultant and therapist at leannenaylor.com

A FINAL THOUGHT

Getting in control of your wealth is the single most important thing you can do to secure your own future.

Sounds a bit profound? Maybe...

But are you really prepared to waste your life waiting for a rich husband or a lottery win?

Relying on someone else's decisions to create your dream life?

How would it feel to know that if you took 3 months off to travel, your bills and costs would be paid and you could completely relax?

What about knowing that if you chose to work less hard in your 50s, you'd still have plenty of money coming in, and be able to pick and choose which clients you took on?

And if I said you could do all this without needing to live by candlelight, eating economy brand baked beans... still buying gin, going on holiday and doing things that make life fun...

How incredible would that be?

Stop telling yourself that you're not good with money, or can't do numbers, or don't like gin... and decide to do something different.

Try a different sort of gin, find a different sort of financial adviser and create a different sort of life – one that feels right for you, whatever that looks like.

Or pop over to my website www.peacetogether.co.uk for loads more great content.

Best wishes

Claire Sweet

FINANCIAL ADVISER & MONEY COACH

ABOUT THE AUTHOR

Claire Sweet is an award-winning Financial Adviser and Money Coach who helps gin-loving business owners to organise their finances and create a wealth plan to grow their assets to £500k or more in the next 3-5 years.

Alongside Peace Together Money Coaching, Claire has worked for fifteen years as a Financial Adviser and a Mortgage and Protection Adviser, helping hundreds of clients to plan for their future retirement, protect their families and buy their dream homes.

Building on her successful career primarily helping high-achieving female coaches and consultants, Claire now supports them on their financial independence journey by

coaching them to maximise their future wealth, without needing to go without holidays and things that make life fun.

She has been featured in a range of publications including The Telegraph, The Guardian, Moneywise and Sheerluxe, as a guest panelist on the Work in Progress podcast and at Courier Live 2019. She was a presenter at Womanifest in 2020 and is regularly asked to speak on BBC Radio Kent as an expert in her field.

Claire lives in the Kent countryside with her husband Phil and enjoys spending time outside with her small herd of 8 alpacas. When she's not working, she loves travelling all over the world, meeting new people and sharing in new adventures.

Claire is available for public speaking events and seminars, as well as 1-2-1 Money Coaching and Regulated Financial Advice.

Message me here >> https://m.me/ClaireSweet01

YouTube >> https://bit.ly/ClaireSweetYouTube

website >> www.peacetogether.co.uk

Printed in Great Britain
by Amazon

80936068R00098